# THE TIME FACTOR

KEVIN MCGRANE

Revised 2017

Copyright © 2017 Kevin McGrane

All rights reserved.

ISBN: 0983650020

ISBN-13: 9780983650027

Library of Congress Control Number: 2011940251

Kevin McGrane

Published by Kevin McGrane

Parts of this book has been Edited by Heidi Connolly,

Harvard Girl Word Services

"The only time you really live fully is from thirty to sixty. The young are slaves to dreams; the old servants of regrets. Only the middle-aged have all their five senses in the keeping of their wits." —Theodore Roosevelt

This book is dedicated to my mother
Patricia Ann McGrane (1936-1997).
Who always had my back and believed that
I was going to make a difference in this world one day.

Did you know that there are 525, 600 minutes in a year, and that after you subtract out sleep and work time, most people have over 200, 000 minutes, or about 40 percent of their time free or off?

But consider this: The U.S. Bureau of Labor Statistics, in its American Time Use Survey conducted in 2015, says that the American civilian population spends only about 16, 500 minutes a year on educational activities!

So, what happened to the other 183, 500 minutes?

Find out in this book...!!

Are you living in someone else's time? Or maybe in a matrix, a simulated reality of past civilizations' clocks and calendar systems?

Are we out of sync with time for the twenty-first century and don't even know it...?

I believe so...

Keep Reading... You decide...

# CONTENTS

# CONTENTS

# ACKNOWLEDGMENTS

This has been mostly a solo journey over these last ten years, as passion and belief have been the driving forces behind this book. As Ben Franklin said, "Energy and persistence conquer all things."

I want to thank my wife Donna, who is one heck of a woman and exemplifies the phrase "just do it." The word "lazy" is not in her vocabulary, or even in her mind.

Special thanks go to Anthony Robbins, whose Personal Power tapes inspired me to change direction in my life one late night back in 1989.

I also want to thank the many great authors and speakers who have helped me stay on track over the years Eckhart Tolle, Dr. Wayne Dyer, Dr. Stephen Covey, Dr. Deepak Chopra, Dr. David R. Hawkins, and David Allen, as well as Jack Canfield "Chicken Soup for the Soul" and Steven Harrison "Best Seller Blueprint Live".

Last but not least, I want to give thanks to all my tax clients. Without them over the past decade and a half, I might not have developed The 1440 Power System®, nor had the data to support some of my work for this book.

www.1440time.com

# ABOUT THIS BOOK

**Factor: An element or cause that contributes to a result**

*The Time* Factor book has been created for:

- People who are looking and are ready for a book that can make a difference in their life right now.
- For people who already think outside the box and are ready to learn about how to Think Outside the Clock™ for an even more fulfilling life.
- People who wish they had more time for any number of reasons—to do chores, have fun, read books, more family time, workout, make additional money, or just be more successful.
- People who have tried everything, but still haven't found the motivational juice with the lasting power to push them into a new state of purpose, gratitude and wakefulness.
- People who need a panacea for the Time's Fault Syndrome (TFS), the world's greatest justification for why we can't do what we want to do, because "no time" gets in the way.

This book is designed to provide information and motivation to our readers. It is sold with the understanding that the publisher is not engaged to render any type of psychological, legal, or any other kind of professional advice. The content is the sole expression and opinion of its author. You are responsible for your own choices, actions, and results.

# PREFACE

What started out as a change in the way I looked at the clock—as I navigated my way through one crazy tax season and the unbelievable year of 2007—has turned out to be a ten-year grand adventure and discovery into the world of time. Little did I know that my life would be transformed forever—and that transformation would be the impetus for creating a whole new way to process time and a patent clock to go along with it!

What do I mean by "a new way to process time"? Let's say you have a friend named Mike, and he is running an online business, and still using an old computer and 56k dial-up speed to access the internet and run his business. How much productivity, energy, money, and *time* do you think he will lose unwittingly if he continues to stay with this archaic method?

Hmm...*Wait a minute, Sherlock. If my friend doesn't know what he doesn't know, then he'll continue to do things the same way because he won't know he's losing anything!*

Exactly, my dear Watson. His perception of things will not change until he knows what he doesn't know! His business will decline as technological advances, and the competition passes him by.

Only when he learns that his computer is outdated and cable, FiOS, and 4G wireless are all available to make his internet speed up to fifty to two hundred times faster—will his company flourish, succeed and have more time to enjoy life.

Is it that Mike is resistant to change, or maybe a procrastinator? Or is it possible Mike just doesn't know what he doesn't know, and if no one says anything about it to him, all's normal…?

Is it possible we're trying to access the world of the 21$^{st}$ century with an outdated time system of thousands of years ago and don't even know it?

If time seems elusive—wish could certainly enjoy more—and it seems to be moving just a little bit too quickly by—read on—and do relax. I have created a *superior Time Awareness System*™ *(TAS)*, including a new way to measure time called **1440TIME**™ that will provide you blazing high-speed access into the 21st century. Showing you how to *"think outside the antiquated linear standard clock"*—as time will slow, flow, and expand, leaving you in control and in charge of the clock.

This isn't some hocus-pocus, some magical affirmation that you repeat, or even close to the traditional standard time management book. The answers are already here, they are just hidden in plain sight.

**"Be not astonished at new ideas; for it is well known to you that a thing does not therefore cease to be true because it is not accepted by many."** —Baruch Spinoza

# INTRODUCTION

"If everyone is thinking alike, then somebody isn't thinking." —George Patton

This book was designed as the ultimate tool for motivation—personal growth and eventual to surpass the current level of time awareness you have right now, but it takes a different approach from other books of this sort that require substantial conscious effort. Why? Because sustained conscious effort is where most people seem to misfire. Blame it on **effortful control** if you want. Effortful control is the ability to regulate one's responses to external stimuli, and since we have plenty of that, with relationships, kids, smart-phones, emails, and the media, no wonder why we can't concentrate for any length of time on some of the most important things in our lives.

This approach may be new and unique, but I believe that all you need is a slight shift in your subconscious to bring you powerful, long-lasting results, and you can do this instinctually, with little or no effort. It's much the same as the way a child learns to ride a bike: After just a few run-a-longs, solo pushes, and perhaps a spill or two, instinct takes over and the feet begin to push the pedals unconsciously—*and once learned you cannot unlearn how to ride a bike.* At this point, the journey down the road of life has begun and there is no turning back.

**The Time Factor** is the blueprint that will help you chart a new way of seeing and doing things in your life immediately. It will correct the chronic delusion of the current standard clock and calendar that pervades the mind unconsciously, having you conforming to an erroneous cadence.

You will see time as a mindset and that when recognized; it becomes your greatest asset of all-time.

I think you'll soon agree that its methods will be the prerequisite for all time management and motivational books on the market today, as these books are missing two ingredients (1440TIME™ and The 1440 Power System®), and we all know what happens when an ingredient has been left out of a recipe.

For those who are ready, *The Time Factor* will take a mere spectator to a significant player—or will take a significant player to one of the best players in the greatest game of all—*the Game of Life*.

I am extremely honored to have this new association with you. That you are reading this material now shows that you are looking for even more in your life. Readers are leaders after all.

Please know that the thoughts I present here are my own, a composite of many years of experiences, drive, passion, and learning from others that have culminated in this simple but powerful message.

Enjoy the book and welcome to the world of real time.

# 1. TIME

**"If today was the last day of your life, what would you do?"** —Steve Jobs

I am the timekeeper, a time planner, a time coach, and a time salesman. In other words, I sell, track and give more time...because who does not want more time? The bonus is that this time is free! Well, maybe not entirely free. The cost of time is that we are each allowed only one full rotation around the Life Clock and only twenty-four hours in each one of those days. Shortly, however, we will explore exactly how we can experience a new **Time Awareness System**™ (TAS) that gives you more time, hence slowing down the Life clock.

This book's premise is that, by challenging our long-held assumptions about time, we can change our lives. This premise is built on the belief that we have been living in the twenty-first century in a way that is fundamentally flawed and out of sync with time as we know it today. Why do I make this statement? Because we are still using the same time system that was used by ancient civilizations, even though it has long been diverging with the world as we know it. It's time to ask: Why are we still using an outdated chronometer modeled by early humans during the times of chariots, mummies, and allegoric gods in the twenty-first century?

The now is all we have and it is all we've ever had. Even though we know this at a deeper level to be true, it seems so hard to stay on track in our fast past world. Our mind is so easily distracted; there is so much to do, so much going on, and so much to hear that we lose sight of the *now*. We get lost and wrapped up in the clock and calendar of our existence—which becomes the *now*. And those series of now's become your story (journey) or even purpose without knowing it. Life has become a chain of time limitations; a sequence of appointments, birthdays, TV shows, holidays, jobs, events, weekends, and ultimately the illusion of time passing by quickly. *Time flies, as we say and hear all the time.*

So, what can we do? How can we slow it down, make it more fulfilling, purposeful, fun, productive, loving, enjoyable, and yes, even more money! There's hope!

*The Time Factor* answers these questions and more, providing a simple but powerful insight into the world of time and money—a new found awareness that will alter your perception of the clock and cash forever.

You will begin the healing process instantly by letting go of the ancient clocks and calendar systems of the past, which lead to the Time's-Fault Syndrome and the Time's-Flying Syndrome, and other time-related stress ailments that have held you back from being more than you can be.

By *"thinking outside the clock,"* I have taken *TIME*—something unappreciated by many, underestimated by plenty, undervalued by most, and misunderstood by nearly all—and broken into a *powerful Time Awareness System™ and motivational tool for personal enhancement.*

What if you could...

- Have more passion in your life?
- Have more time in a day?
- Make more money?
- Be in control of time instead of at its mercy?
- Minimize time-related stress, which is said to speed up the aging process and slow the blood flow to the brain?
- Increase your daily personal productivity?
- Read and learn more (now that you have the time)?
- Become more physically fit (part of the ultimate equation for living a healthier, longer, and more vigorous life)?
- Rid yourself of the Time's Fault Syndrome forever?

Being rich in time is the most important step toward having a gratifying and fulfilling life. And frankly, it's about time that we all raise our standards for our children's future, our future, and our country's future. If not now, when?

I will have succeeded in my goal if, once you have read this book, you have been enriched with a *newfound appreciation* and *awareness of time*, the *greatest gift of all*.

From here on, what you do with your new appreciation of time and its great power is in your hands.

**"I may not be rich in money yet, but I am rich in time now."** —Kevin McGrane

# 2. THE TICKET INTO THE GAME

**"Life is a ticket to the greatest show on earth."**
—Martin H. Fischer

```
┌ ─ ─ ─ ─ ─ ─ ─ ─ ─ ─ ─ ─ ─ ─ ─ ─ ─ ─ ┐
│              ADMIT                  │
│               ONE                   │
│         LIFE TIME TICKET            │
│                                     │
└ ─ ─ ─ ─ ─ ─ ─ ─ ─ ─ ─ ─ ─ ─ ─ ─ ─ ─ ┘
```

Time is our entrance into the Great Game of Life. If it came in the form of a ticket, we'd get only one, and without it, we would not be here to create, play, love, learn, laugh, or see the world. We could not appreciate life's beauty or even lament its limitations. By making time into a scapegoat and attributing to it characteristics it does not really have, we shape and mask reality. We constantly use time for a plethora of reasons, excuses, and platitudes: "I don't have the time." "There isn't enough time." "When I have some time, I will start." But time is not to blame! It has never been the reason; it is not the enemy. In fact, time is the greatest ally and most magnanimous tool ever.

Although this book will help just about anybody (even my four-teen-year-old twin girls are successfully applying its tenets in their daily lives), it is primarily written for the millions who are age thirty-five to sixty-five—those who compose the financial engine of America and need to mobilize their will to become organized and take immediate action, as this age group has the power, size and income to implement change now, if they can only find the time…! In addition, most individuals in this phase of life (including yours truly), time appears to be picking up the pace. At thirty-five where did the twenties go? Forty-five flies by. Getting to fifty is a blur. And the over-sixty stage is here in a blink. Is there a reason why time felt as if it went more slowly when we were younger, even though nothing has really changed since then? If there are the exact numbers of hours in a day now as there were twenty, thirty, and fifty years ago, how can time possibly be different?

If, like me, you think it's just that "time flies," or you believe "you never have time anymore" because you're busier than you were as a child, well, you're probably right —but it's only part of the equation.

Consider this example. You're in traffic, in a hurry because you're late for work. You sit there for ten minutes swearing. Time drags on and on. Finally, there is movement, and slowly but surely you drive through the scene of the fender bender only to notice the traffic has been caused by people slowing to see what happened.

Now let's look at the same scenario a different way. You're in the same traffic not late, and you're listening to something educational you like, or listening to music, and drinking a latte. The same ten or fifteen minutes pass by—in fact, time *flies* by, and before you know it you're cruising through the intersection.

What's the difference? You haven't even noticed the minutes that went by because you were busy now with your other experiences and thoughts. It was your *perception* that changed, not the circumstances. Or have you ever noticed how long it takes to drive somewhere that you have never been before, and the ride home seems much faster.

We've all experienced the illusion of having time slow down or speed up. Sometimes the clock drags on and sometimes the clock flies by. Imagining being able to control the speed of time, or at least managing the perception of it! What if we were able to change the perception of time (the clock) at will, and use this new awareness as a tool to help us manage time in a new exciting way?

As you begin to grasp the concepts of this book, you will gain a new appreciation and a renewed awareness of time. This heightened awareness will ignite your passion and enable you to do anything you truly desire.

Are you about to start another week stuck at a job that just pays the bills, or a livelihood that has you doing what you love?

Are you about to start another week with the same old same old, or maybe a week that has you one-step closer to a goal you set some time ago?

Are you about to start another week and ask where did that week-end go, or a week that has you pumped, a bit exhausted from a great weekend, but exhilarated about what's to come this week?

Or maybe you are already doing it; loving life, making the money you want, feeling physically fit, enjoying family, friends, and traveling to some great places, but you just want more time or wish you could slow it down.

It doesn't matter where you are currently, or where you want to go—one thing is for sure though, we get only one ticket into this life here on earth and only so much time to *live it*...

## TIME IGNORANCE

The first thing to understand is that many suffer from, and need to overcome what I call *Time Ignorance*. Time Ignorance is the automatic by-product of the internal clock mechanism that we inherit at birth. Because this ignorance about the true nature of time is an embedded belief, and since changing an old belief can be tough, the ideas presented in this book are here to help you grasp it.

The excuse that you don't have enough time and that it's time's fault will shortly be blown out of the water. It's time to say goodbye to blaming time...forever.

*The Time Factor* is a book written for immediate use! This means that as far as time is concerned, no further study will be needed. Once time is viewed and internalized as it is presented in this book, I can assure you that you will never see time the same way again.

So, come aboard and enjoy the ride. The cost is small, but the time you will gain is priceless.

**"I cannot teach anybody anything; I can only make them think."** —Socrates

# 3. TIME, INSIDE A MATRIX?

**"Some things have to be believed to be seen."**
—Ralph Hodgson

Is time really moving faster these days? Was time slower when you were younger? Is the pace of life (think of it as the speed of time) out of control? Do you want more time in a day? Do you wish you could slow down your months and years? Are you living on someone else's time clock, or maybe living your life in a matrix, a simulated reality from past civilizations' clocks and calendar systems?

"Matrix—1. something that constitutes the place or point from which something else originates, takes form, or develops: the Greco-Roman world was the matrix for Western civilization." –Dictionary. com

Do your old beliefs, your sports team, your music idols, your job, your social networks, print and TV media, TV shows, Hollywood, and other hypnotic time distractions have you no longer questioning your own journey—and on cruise control?

Let's start by looking at what we know about time and what we perceive it to be.

Time is really nothing more than a word in our minds! As soon as we think the word, up pops an association with a place we have to be, an appointment we have to keep, or something we have to do. Maybe we get a flash of it from old photos and songs from the past—"the good ol' days." Or perhaps the word calls to mind the lines on our face, the upcoming wedding of a daughter or son, or a vacation we can't wait for in the spring.

Time and the passage of time mean different things to different people. But we can all agree that the pendulum of time keeps on tickin', one second at a time. Just as the pendulum swings back and forth, so do we, as we think about the past, then the future, then the past again. In a nutshell, it seems we're leaving out the only time that really matters: the moment in the here and now.

We all know the expression, "time is money." Or is it money that buys time? Either way, we all know what these words mean, none of us ever believe we have enough of either time or money. We have debt and time for social networking, YouTube and TV, but many aren't physically fit, because we have no time. Countless do not read enough quality material because they have not enough time, but have plenty of time to watch sports, and our learning has diminished vastly in this country, because apparently, we have not the time.

So you see **time** is the culprit, and the old 12-hour clock handed down long…long…ago, along with its partner in crime the **calendar**, has most predisposed to time-related dis-ease in the 21st century, without even knowing it…*!*

**"Know or listen to those who know."**
—Baltasar Gracian

## NEWS ALERT!, 2015

*Nielsen reports that in 2008–2009, TV viewing hit an all-time high, as Americans spent an average of almost five hours a day in front of the TV, up 20 percent from ten years before. Moreover, roughly 40 percent of tablet and smartphone owners in the U.S. used their devices daily while watching TV in 2011.* That amount of time is close to eight years of college, over 100,000 minutes a year watching television, which represents about 20 percent of your time, since there are 525,600 minutes in one year.

That was eight years ago, in 2017 the average is down slightly to 4 hours and 51 minutes, but now more time is spent online with social media and our smart phones!!

The purpose and outcome of this book are to activate your **Time Awareness System**™ and have written this book knowing that people process information differently, and as such, have combined altered strategies to be able to deliver it broadly.

**"Make your life a mission—not an intermission."**
—Arnold H. Glasgow

## NEWS ALERT JULY 2017

*comScore mobile metrix, U.S. Age 18+, Dec 2013 – Dec 2016 spend average of 2 hours and 51 minutes per day on their mobile, or about 153,738 minutes per year! I heard Facebook aggregate users spend about 10.5 billion minutes a day excluding mobile.*

*Source http://www.cnbc.com/2016/02/04/facebook-turns-12--trillions-in-time-wasted.html*

**Hmmm… So, it seems that we do have plenty of time. Or don't we?**

Let's compare that to one human life, which is approximately 40 million minutes long!

77 years x 525,600 = 40,471,200

Remember, we only get one ticket per lifetime and 365 days a year to play in the game.

**"No snowflake in the avalanche ever feels responsible"** —Voltaire

## PUT TIME TO WORK FOR YOU

Since time and money are part of this book, I'd like you to start to think of the internet in the way you might think about interest on the dollar: that it's either working for you or against you. Most of us know full well that credit card interest work against us. We also know that in general, interest rates on CDs (certificates of deposit) or savings accounts (at least in times when rates are better than they are now!) work for us.

Is it just a coincidence that these two sets of circumstances are happening at the same time—that from our government to the masses, the country is riddled in trillions of dollars of interest debt, but we manage to spend trillions of minutes surfing the Internet, watching television, and "wasting" the time we have at our disposal? I don't think so.

**"You cannot change your destination overnight, but you can change your direction overnight."** —Jim Rohn

Quick, how many <u>letter f</u>'s are there in this sentence below?

**Finished Files are the results of years of scientific study combined with the experience of years.**

Time's up! The answer is...?

If you have done this exercise before, you know the point. If you haven't, you may have counted three, four, or five "f's"—instead of the six there really are. Why? Because the subconscious mind tends to delete the "f" in scientific, or ignore one or more of the "f's" in the three "of" words.

What's the point? Think about how many other things in our lives we could be missing, even though they may be obvious and plain to see?

Could it be that time is the mind's grandest illusion of all time?

Could it be that we are currently living in a two or three "f" world when there are much more if we just looked a little deeper or from a different angle?

Like the ego the current standard clock is not wrong, it's just a limited and distorted view of time.

**"Perception is strong and sight weak."**
—Miyamato Musahi

# 4. RIGHT PLACE—WRONG TIME

**"The future is here. It's just not widely distributed yet."** —William Gibson

It seems to me that things in our world are more than a little bit off these days, that we are out of tune and out of touch, and that our predicament has been building for some years. Sure, we could blame the government, Wall Street, the media, reality TV, the smartphone, the tablet, and the economy, but maybe the real question is whether we the people, are simply thinking and living in a paradigm that no longer works. I heard a reporter on a recent newscast who might agree. He said, "The boomers changed the world; now the world is changing them."

The Industrial Revolution is over in this country. Yes, it's true that it worked for over two hundred years, but you cannot build another Manhattan, have another housing boom like we had in the 60's, 70's and 80's pacing the boomers, or have another World War II to create jobs building tanks, planes, and jeeps. We can look forward to the day when electric cars, solar and wind power, fuel cells, and our abundant natural gas reserves will be utilized effectively, while employing millions with long-term job security. But in the meantime, waiting is not an intelligent strategy.

We are in the early stages of the Communication and Information Age in the twenty-first century, or is it the Age of Expectation? **Thinking is the new game in town**, anticipating change is the strategy, and your mind, the net, and your time are the tools—and not as much the hands, hammer, and shovel.

It is said that Neanderthals became extinct because they didn't do a good enough job anticipating change, adapting to the new world, as the Cro-Magnons did by strategizing and making technological advances. In effect, Cro-Magnons left the Neanderthals in the dust, where they suffered the fate of extinction. Are we heading down the same path as the Neanderthals by not anticipating change, by living an old paradigm— even as the world rapidly evolves right before our eyes, passes us by because our old belief systems from the past have us blinded to the truth?

Look around. What do you see? Financial disparity and politicians stuck in egoic battles, paralyzed by pride. Millions of people not working, yet have a sound mind and body. I see a country that has more issues and divisions than ever before. Yes, we need change, but are those in charge now going to be given a chance?

**"Education is a progressive discovery of our own ignorance."** —Will Durant

Has the primitive clock and calendar finally run its useful life? Has it been fully depreciated after thousands of years of use?

Are we in a transitional period where we're caught between old Industrial Age thinking and the new Communication and Information Age thinking, but still coasting on the residue from a world past—a time gone by?

Are we twenty-first-century Neanderthals, continuing to choose unconsciousness rather than recognizing the world has changed and will continue to change, all the while standing around waiting for the ice to thaw?

Time keeps rolling on and technology keeps rolling out faster than the old standard clock can keep up with. We should be consistently embracing change, forward thinking and new ideas. The old tried and true of the past is just that, the past. **And the past doesn't equal the future.** What's it going to take hyperinflation, food shortages, gas lines, civil unrest, or even worse?

Be an observer of the delusional thinking that is upon us. Be aware and think outside of what you are seeing, and have a plan A, B and C. Remember TIME stands for **Things I Must Earn!**

**"It is not the strongest of the species that survive, nor the most intelligent, but the one most responsive to change."** —Clarence Darrow

# 5. THE SUN, THE MOON, AND THE PLANETS

Time has been studied by great minds from Copernicus (1473–1543) to Galileo (1564–1642), from Newton (1643–1727) to Einstein (1879–1955), and to the modern-day Stephen Hawking in his book *A Brief History of Time*. And though physics is a fascinating science and you will hear its overtones throughout this book, what we are talking about is much, much more. We are looking for the secret of time in a place available to each one of us right now.

Thousands of years ago, our ancestors used the night sky, along with other means such as the water clock and the sundial, to estimate the passage of time. The nights were full of danger, darkness, and cold, while the day's sun brought light, warmth, safety, and hope. Knowing when to plant the crops in the spring so the harvest would be plentiful in the fall meant survival through the harsh winter months. There was no smartphone, TV, Applebee's, and no www. A night out at the movies was a front row seat in the universe's arena, the night sky, watching the phases of the moon, the close planets, and the stars constantly rotating and providing help to navigate through the seasons of time. Did people then ponder the mysteries inherent in the world around them? Perhaps. Perhaps not. All we really know is that it was a way to capture the essence of time as a tool for survival.

It comes as no surprise, then, that our calendar and clock system is based on the Earth's revolution around the sun and the moon's monthly cycle. Early civilizations used the same measurements to tell time, but without the sophisticated equipment we have today, like radar and satellites. For example, it was over three thousand years ago that the Egyptians decided to divide the day from sunrise to sunset into twelve parts. Was this a good idea? Sure, at least back then. But this clock tells you **time today**, it is not a measurement of time!? Imagine if we measured time? Is our current clock system still valid for twenty-first-century men and women, outside the farmers and fishermen?

Life was different then! So was the way people viewed time. But most people today don't give time much thought—outside of their addiction and adherence to the tick-tocking of the twelve-hour mechanical clock system that has been handed down through the generations. As Deepak Chopra says, "most people are trapped in the hypnosis of social conditioning."

Greek mythology gave us Chronos, the god of linear time. The Romans gave us June for Juno, an ancient goddess; July and August from Julius and Augustus Caesar; March for Mars, the ancient god of war; and January for Janus, the god of opening and closing doors. The Northern Germanic tribes gave us the Norse gods: Tyr for Tuesday, Woden for Wednesday, Frigg for Friday, Thor the god of thunder, for Thursday. Interesting, yes, but times have changed, you think?

In Latin, September means "seven," but September is our calendar's ninth month; October, from the Latin *octo*, means "eight," but October is our calendar's tenth month. November comes from *novem* or "nine," but is our eleventh month, and December comes from *decem* or "ten," but is our twelfth month. In fact, the reason for these discrepancies is that Caesar added in a month of his own just because he could, as did his nephew Augustus, who followed him.

Does this mean that we should use the same calendar, the one developed by the powerful of others, centuries ago?

Furthermore, our seven-day week comes from the seven most visible planets to man: The Sun, Moon, Mercury, Venus, Mars, Saturn, and Jupiter. They are just ancient beliefs and words from a time long past, systems created and changed over the years by the ancient or powerful of the moment to quantify time, likely implemented as a way to control the herd to pay their debts and taxes.

The word calendar is derived from the Latin *calendarium*, meaning an interest or account book, and is related to the Latin word *kalend*, meaning "I cry!" (From *The Origins of Our Modern Calendar* by Linda Kerr). Debts were due and these books kept track of who paid and owed.

In fact, many of our words and systems are based on a time long past. Yes, these systems have been tweaked over the years to make them palatable by current standards, but at what cost? Are we being controlled by our quantification of time? Are we being herded by and old clock and calendar in a way that actually is serving others, or maybe the powerful of today? Is our brain still calibrated to a time when information traveled by days and months, in a world of seconds and minutes today?

**"Be mindful of how you approach time. Watching the clock is not the same as watching the sun rise."** —Sophia Bedford-Pierce

# 6. THE TRILOGY OF TIME

**"What happens depends on our way of observing it or on the fact that we observe it."**
—Werner Heisenberg

As we start moving further along the path on our journey of time for the twenty-first century, you will notice that your **Time Awareness System**™ (TAS) is becoming activated. Once this happens, you will note that you are beginning to think about time differently. This is where our journey into time begins in earnest.

**The Trilogy of Time is the basis for the book**—it is comprised of three components:

> ➤ **The Life Clock**
> ➤ **1440TIME**™**/The 1440 Power System**®
> ➤ **The Compound Value of Time**

Each element serves its own unique purpose, but when all are aligned, your life will flow easier, it has too...

The Trilogy starts with the work of a wonderful artist and creative soul from Paris, France. I found Bertrand Planes while I was working on this book at the time, via his unique website (bertrandplanes.com), and he and I have become friends over the years.

It is Bertrand Planes who created the Life Clock from the typical clock with which we now keep time. Bertrand Planes' Life Clock, however, is different in that it illustrates time over the course of one's life (from age zero to eighty-four), as shown below.

## THE LIFE CLOCK

With Bertrand's permission, I have expanded on his concept of the Life Clock, which is an important element in the Trilogy of Time. The purpose of the Life Clock is to serve as your own personal GPS. It does this by showing you exactly where you are on the great Time Clock of Life in terms of life expectancy. Later, you'll see where you are on the Time Clock of Life when it is segmented into four quarters of time.

The Life Clock allows you to see the big picture of where you have been, where you are now, and what's left on the Game Clock of Life. It enables you to mobilize awareness, gratitude, and appreciation for everything—for all that is included in what I call the Context of Life.

**"The only thing some people do is get older."**
—Edgar Watson Howe

The second element of the Trilogy is 1440TIME™/The 1440 Power System®, which is what I call the *Content of Life*. This is where you make it happen, or you don't, also referred to as Equal Opportunity Time **(EOT)**. It is this element that teaches us to use it smartly and control our perception of time for our own advantage by slowing it down or speeding it up. In this paradigm, each day is seen as 1,440 minutes (60 minutes x 24 hours = 1,440)—no more and no less, and each day is further divided into three zones of time in the day: **Sleep—Livelihood—On-Time**

By doing this we're further breaking down the days (1440 minutes) into smaller units or zones. Whatever zone you're in becomes the present, and when your attention is fully engaged in the present, that zone's power is transformed and magnified. More on this later in chapter 16.

Minutes

Hours – "Just Say No"

**"Take care of the minutes and the hours will take care of themselves."** —Lord Chesterfield

I think Lord Chesterfield was exactly right. Even though he wrote these words in the 1800s, the sentiment works just as well today as it did back then.

The third element of our Time Trilogy is what I call the Compound Value of Time, based on Einstein's Eighth Wonder of the World concept: the power of compounding interest as related to money. In this case, however, we are relating it to the compounding of **minutes of time over time**. Look at the example below showing the power of compounding; even though it's not illustrating Einstein's power of compound interest, you'll get the point.

Would you rather choose to have $2,000 a day for the next twenty days, or $2 a day for the next twenty days that compound each day by doubling the amount? Let's do the math. $2,000 a day for twenty days equals $40,000. $2 a day for twenty days compounded by doubling each day equals over $1,000,000! The answer is clear!

The Compound Value of Time works much in the same way; it's the daily minutes compounded over time that goals, dreams and successes manifest, and is the third element of the Trilogy of Time.

**"Compound interest is the eighth wonder of the world. He who understands it, earns it…he who doesn't…pays it."** —Albert Einstein

## THE TRILOGY OF TIME

- The Life Clock (GPS)
- The 1440 Power System®
- The Compound Value of Time

*"The First Wonder of the Universe"*

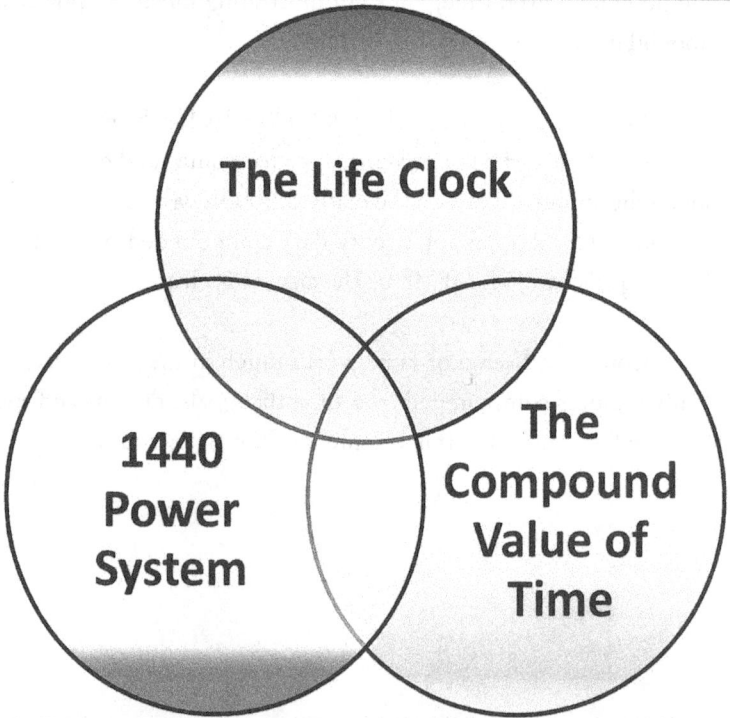

**The Life Clock**

**1440 Power System**

**The Compound Value of Time**

**"The soul never thinks without a mental picture."** —Aristotle

## The Time Awareness System™
(TAS)

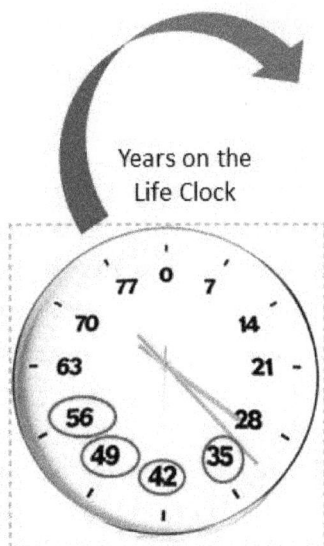

### The Daily Clock
**The 1440 Power System®**

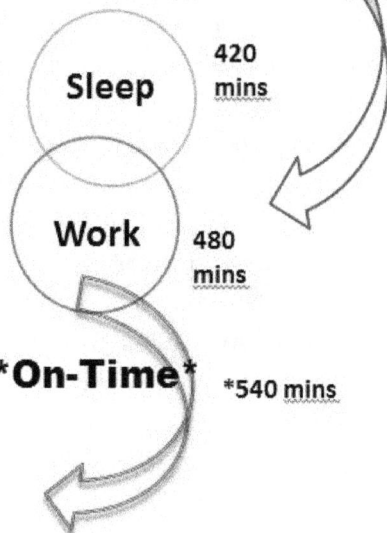

Years on the
Life Clock

Sleep — 420 mins

Work — 480 mins

*The Compound Value of Time

*On-Time* — *540 mins

It is in the *On-Time minutes on the daily clock compounded where dreams are made!

"Know how to live the time that is given you."
—Dario Fo

## THINKING OUTSIDE THE BOX

*Every time you have thought, you make a chemical, if you condition the body over twenty years with the same chemicals, you're conditioning the mind like a servant or an animal, which becomes* **the state of being as the way we define ourselves.**

*A habit is when the body becomes the mind—the change is to pull the mind out of the body, and to put it back in the brain, which takes an active will. If we can't think greater than we feel, then we will never change. When you learn new information and knowledge—new circuits and new connections develop in the brain—called thinking outside the box. The greatest habit we have to break is the habit of being ourselves.*

Dr. Joe Dispenza D.C. Evolve Your Brain: The Science of Changing Your Mind

*The key here is to think outside the box by* **thinking outside the clock!**

The **Time Awareness System**™ accomplishes this by using time itself to bring you present (the now). By breaking the agreement (the autonomous activity you have with the standard clock and calendar) the separation has begun, and true time awareness is activated. Once activated it cannot be rescinded.

**"Most people are other people. Their thoughts are someone else's opinions, their lives a mimicry, their passions a quotation."**
—Oscar Wilde

# 7. IF YOU'RE TOO CLOSE TO THE TREES YOU WON'T SEE THE FOREST

**"Discovery consists of looking at the same thing as everyone else and thinking something different."** —Albert Szent-Gyorgyi

Once upon a time, until about ten years ago, I was too close to the trees to see the forest. When I discovered how my perception was clouding my abilities, I made a simple change in the way I looked at the clock. This led to a whole new way of thinking and living. It was a serendipitous moment when suddenly my view went from microscopic to macroscopic. I finally began seeing what was beyond the trees: the forest for as far as the eye could see. It was a tremendous feeling, one that still fills my life today. For once you see it, you will always see it; it never goes away.

What is this metaphorical forest, and how did I change my thinking? It started with the way I thought about time itself back in the 2007 tax season, and everything else followed. The trees in this analogy represent our current and outdated way of calibrating time using the twelve-hour standard clock and our seven-day-a-week calendar. The forest (and beyond) is our new up-to-date, corrected version of time, based on the **Life Clock and the 1,440 minutes we have available to us every single day.**

Remember that we are challenging an assumption that has been with us forever, at least as far as time as we know it is concerned.

When we use the Time Trilogy, we force our brains to fire new thoughts and new chemicals and to make new nerve cell connections. Ultimately, we will change a lifetime of social conditioning and our perception of our clock, our calendar, and time itself! By doing this, we can break the old pattern of how we see time (*the trees*), which is merely a subconscious or conditioned response taught to us—and add a new conscious pattern-*Time Awareness* (the forest). This implies that you're not only conscious of the standard clock and calendar, but you're also conscious of the totality of time itself, **which is you're born, get 1440 minutes every day until some finite time in the future, hopefully into the 80's, 90's or 100's.**

It's time to break through the structured mechanical time standard of the past, and move you to a new premium time model for 2017 and beyond, **as modern times, need a modern time.**

Being alive right now in the 21$^{st}$ century is worth every minute and then some…So why not have more of it and slow it down!?

On the next page, you will see a simple illustration that represents how we use our current time system (the trees) based on a centuries-old system, and then a different way to look at time (the forest), using the Life Clock, 1440TIME™ and the 1440 Power System®.

**"If you have zest and enthusiasm you attract zest and enthusiasm. Life does give back in kind".** —Norman Vincent Peale

| | |
|---|---|
| Ancient Clock | 21st Century Time Clock |
| The Trees | The Forest and Beyond |
| Twelve-Hour Standard Clock | The Life Clock (GPS) |

| | |
|---|---|
| Calendarium | The 1440 Power System® |

| | |
|---|---|
| Janus, Julius, Augustus, Mars | 1,440 Minutes |

Is your view being limited? Is the old standard clock and calendar controlling your perception of time, allowing only a surface level view?

The trees like the twelve-hour mechanical clock and calendar being so close to our everyday lives have us on an automatic pilot, like a drone, responding unconsciously to old systems and words from the ages; however, used in the 21st century as a social conditioning ruse. Governing the masses to act, feel, and respond in certain ways, such as the way people react to the word Friday versus Monday, Saturday versus Tuesday, or a holiday versus any normal workday. **In the world of real-time, there are just 1440 minutes a day, which is one full day on the great clock of your life!**

What if we reprogrammed our minds to think in terms of only the Life Clock and the 1440 minutes we have daily, and used the old current system just as a tool for convenience and conformity? How much more passion would resonate from our being? How much more enthusiasm would emanate out of the doings? How much better could our lives be?

Remember, part of the mind is completely conditioned by our past. This ancient time system (inherited as truth) has taken ownership and is running most lives subconsciously!

The **Time Awareness System**™ breaks that old agreement you have with the current standard clock and calendar—by using the Life Clock and the 1440 Power System® to awaken your inner consciousness. The Life Clock, if seen wisely, increases the intrinsic value of time one hundred-fold, and The 1440 Power System® has your underlying energy flowing with enthusiasm and purpose, as time becomes organized and available.

**"Time was God's first creation."** —Walter Lang

# 8. THAT WOULD BE NOW, PLEASE!

**"The future comes one day at a time."**
—Dean Gooderham Acheson

Getting from point A to point B in the least amount of time and money is what most of us want, whether we're trying to meet a goal, advance our education, travel, or accomplish our chores—especially here in the states over the last ten years. We have grown into a culture that wants it **now**. Our conditioned responses are set to the tune of smart phones, Twitter, text messages, email, Quick Pick Lotteries, fifteen-minute abs, rapid weight-loss schemes, speed dating, packaged instant meals, and the champion, **fast food joints.**

All we have to do is listen to our kids. "I'm bored, Mom, I have nothing to do." Meanwhile they have, video and online computer games, DVD players, iPods, iphones, Kindles, books, NOOKs®, bikes, toys, skateboards, swing sets, pools, pets, and the big HD TV with hundreds of stations to fill their time, and they still have time to be bored!

But if you look at kids' behavior more closely, they'll show you how to be fully present, even though they can drive you nuts with their lack of patience. They want it now, this minute; the present moment, and in reality, it is the only one we truly have.

Today we think in terms of clock time for everything that means work-time, drive-time, appointment time, free-time, family-time, play-time, game-time, down-time, TV time, and bedtime. It is hard for most to think any other way. This time is known as chronological time, which comes from Chronos, the ancient God of measurable time or captain clock, as Jay Griffiths says in her book, A Sideways Look at Time. This is not to say that our current clock and calendar system is worthless. After all, we need a system to regulate our appointments, holidays, birthdays, anniversaries, and to pay our taxes... But I am suggesting a new measurement of time, **1440TIME**™.

Get off Pavlov's clock. It's corrupted with an outdated time program—slowing us down and tainting the processing speed of our brain, like computer malware. This clock causes acute stress, tension, irritable driving syndrome, impatience, and can even bring on a lethargic view of life disorder. Join the 1440 club™, slow it all down, do more, and have extra time to enjoy life's experience.

*"Time, as we experience it, is a physiological event, a concept that we have invented, to explain our experience of change, programmed by our past beliefs, between inheriting from our parents and our indoctrination by society."*
—*Deepak Chopra, The Higher Self*

# 9. THE LIFE CLOCK

**The Life Clock**                    **1440 TIME™**

The Life Clock represents the allotted time over the course of our life, based on seven-year intervals and a life expectancy of eighty-four. Though currently a little lower for both men and women, we're using the age of eighty-four as the benchmark because it is one full rotation around Bertrand Planes' Life Clock. Here, the movement on Planes' Life Clock has been slowed down 61,320 times, so that the minute markers are now measured in years, and the clock is calibrated to measure the age of a person, shown by the numbers zero to eighty-four. The Life Clock gives us a clear visual of our estimated allotted time in this life. In acting as your personal GPS, the Life Clock is meant to show you where **you are in** your life's journey in relation to the eighty-four life expectancy benchmark—not my journey or anyone else's, **the Context of Life**.

It is no wonder why the turtle is in no particular rush to burn through the 1,440 minutes it has each day.

Our turtle's beverage represents our Life's Content, the 1440 minutes you have every day, his cup is the Context, the life clock. Without the cup, there is no-thing to hold the Content in. We need them both.

The most important thing to remember is that **our minutes create our future** and that **time is finite** in the world as we know it. Once we accept that there is no getting more time, and that there is nothing we can do to change the ticking of the current clock, or get any of the past ticks back, it becomes evident that we alone are accountable for where we are now, where we've been, and ultimately how our journey unfolds. As illustrated on the coming page, the Life Clock is divided into four quadrants representing four quarters of life and time: ages zero to twenty-one, twenty-one to forty-two, forty-two to sixty-three, and sixty-three to eighty-four.

When you look at life through Bertrand's clock, you start seeing the forest or context, including your past, your present, and your future. In so doing, this will help activate your Time Awareness System™. When this happens, time becomes tangible, finite, and more than just a number on a clock, a yearly calendar, or a date on a newspaper—it puts time in its proper prospective, recognition at the conscious level, called *time awareness.*

What a great concept Bertrand Plane's Life clock is and wondered why he created it, so I asked him, he said *"Kevin, it was a way to show people visually how fleeting and precious time really is."*

**The Life Clock-1440TIME™/The 1440 Power System®
and The Compound Value of Time** (the trilogy) are the new tools
and methods to assist people in finding passion, purpose, enthusiasm,
and to inspire you from within to go for more, all while enjoying this
great ride of life we've been all blessed with here on earth.

The aim of this book is to do whatever it takes to activate your
Time Awareness System™ (TAS), and once activated it can't be deactivated, even though the old, once powerful standard clock and calendar will try to win you back. It will be impossible.

**1440TIME™** is the most effective time system ever devised: It
not only breaks the current emotional patterns you have tied to the
current clock and calendar, but also uses the power of leveraging minutes, and as you will soon see 1440TIME™ works in a declining fashion, to create a slight sense of urgency, as time counts down throughout the day, hence making it more valuable.

http://the1440powersystem.blogspot.com/2014/10/1440time-
first-prototype.html

**"Time: a paradox, always there, intangible, easy
to overlook, underappreciated, constant, never
ending, yet gone forever and final."**
—Kevin R. McGrane

# THE FOUR QUARTERS OF THE LIFE CLOCK

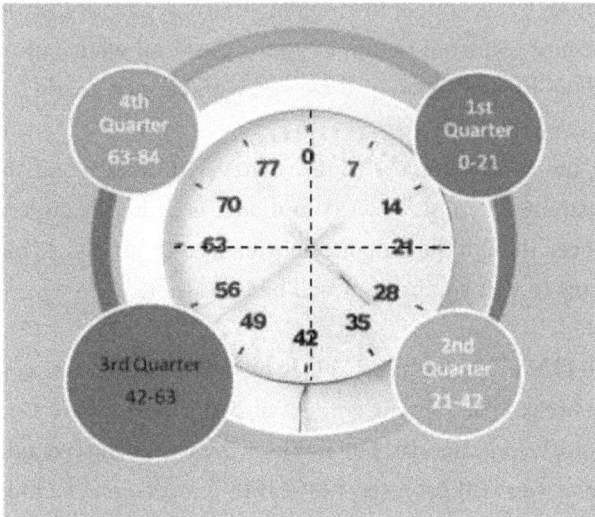

The Life Clock helps you see what time it is *for you* in relation to time over its entirety. Even though it's based on a life expectancy of eighty-four years, (*slightly higher than the actual number today*) it serves the same purpose. We also know that approximately fifty percent of us will live longer than that and fifty percent will not. How we live inside our 1440 minutes every day (*the content*) will either greatly enhance or greatly reduce our chance of being here longer than eighty-four years, (*the context*). When you see life from this slant, it brings time to the forefront of our awareness. We can see glimpses of our childhood, memories of our teen years, and experiences of our twenties. We recall what we learned in our thirties and relive the way we ran through our forties, sped through our fifties, and blinked through our sixties. Maybe, just maybe, we finally learn to appreciate time in our seventies. Better late than never…

Why does it take so long to appreciate time for what it is, the greatest and rarest gift of all?

*As an older client of mine once said to me, "Kevin, we get old too soon and smart too late."*

How many people do you know, maybe it's you, that never seem to get around to doing what you really want to do "I'll get to it tomorrow" or "someday very soon". Paul Coelho, the great Brazilian lyricist and novelist said it perfectly.

*One day you will wake up and there won't be any more time to do the things you've always wanted. Do it now.*

You can start today, I mean right now…No matter what time it is for you on the life clock! It doesn't matter if you have no money. It doesn't matter if you're over weight! It doesn't matter if you have no job! It doesn't matter that you haven't exercised in a long while! It doesn't matter you haven't read a book in twelve years! SO WHAT!!!

Think like a turtle… Slow and steady wins the race… Enjoy and maximize the 1440 minutes you have each day to the fullest, and get started today… You don't have to wait anymore. Your time is now, that's why you found this book. Maybe you weren't ready last week, or when you were in your $2^{nd}$ quarter, but today, right now you are. It's the third quarter! It's your time to shine…

**"The secret of genius is to carry the spirit of the child into old age, which means never losing your enthusiasm."** —Aldous Huxley

## HUMAN NAVIGATION SYSTEM

Millions of us have GPS in our vehicles. Global Positioning Systems are used for directions, golf, walking, hunting, boating, fishing, hiking and more. They give us a sense of control, ease, and knowing; they allow us to track our mileage and find out how long our journey will take; they help us avoid traffic jams and know the distance to that par three. The technology is here to stay. Not only affordable, but when used properly, a GPS can add value to our lives and even more important, can save us valuable time in a day.

What if we look at time similar to the GPS, and use the **Time Awareness System**™ (TAS) as our own human GPS?

▼ **Where you are right now on the Great Clock of Life and where you want go with it…**

**1440TIME**™ **to get you there easier, faster and on time…**

See next page.

## THE GPS AND THE TAS ARE SIMILAR.

Check out the comparisons between below:

## GPS

- Where are you now?
- Where are you going?
- How far are you going?
- How fast you want to get there (via plane, car, or train)?

## TAS

- Where are you on the Life Clock now?
- Where do you want to go with your time?
- How far do you want to go with it?
- How fast do you want to go to get there?
  A. The 1440 Power System®
  B. The Compound Value of Time

For now, it's enough to realize the following:

1. The **Life Clock** is your very own GPS relative to life expectancy.
2. **1440TIME**™ looks at each day as a compilation of 1,440 individual declining minutes, versus the old paradigm of the twelve-hour standard clock.
3. The **Compound Value of Time** acts the same way that the power of compounding has on money, noted by Einstein as the "eighth wonder of the world."

# 10. THE 1440 POWER SYSTEM® 😎

You may never have counted them, but there are 1,440 minutes in a day! The difference for me is that when I look at this number, that's all I see. I don't see "time" or "time flying" or "time being wasted." I simply see 1, 440 minutes that repeat each day, every day. To me, a Tuesday is the same as a Saturday, and a Monday is the same as a Sunday. This is the first step in the utilization of The 1,440 Power System®— ultimately leading to full activation of your Time Awareness System™ **"TAS"**, *presence without thought*. Once this innovation paradigm shift is made, a new mindfulness and a different way to experience time truly unfold. One of the many fringe benefits will be your productivity is bound to increase—whether it's personal (free-time) or job-related it won't' matter, as they both reside in The 1,440 Power System®. The only reason it would not is, *you choose* to revert back to the old standard clock way of thinking, and *thinking is not the same as awareness*. Another fringe benefit will be "TIME SLOWS", or so it seems, how cool is that? The new 1440 Premium Clock shown on the next page works in a unique way—*countdown fashion*, much like a clock the farmers live by, beginning at sunrise (daylight) and working until sunset (darkness), and to this day one of the most productive people on the planet. Do farmers need a clock to tell them what time work is done, or the name of a day of the week *Saturday,* to say it's an off day? I don't think so. The sun's natural daily rise and decline are their time clock. 1440TIME™ works much in the same way, except instead of the sun's movement from light to darkness, it encompasses one entire earth day of time.

When you wake up, the standard clock says 6:00 am, but the 1440TIME™ says **1080**, an entirely new way for the brain to compute and calibrate time.

## THE NEW 1440 CLOCK™

As you take in the new premium time clock concept, remember it is not replacing the old standard clock as we know it just yet. That will take some time and maybe some tweaking, but someday I'm sure it will take over. For now, the 1440CLOCK™ will be primarily be used for Time Awareness Activation—cure Times Fault Syndrome (TFS)—create more time in your day—increase personal productivity, and slow time down...

**"Things don't change. You change your way of looking, that's all".** —Carlos Castaneda

"Time" is one of the most common nouns in the English language, and time is defined in physics as a "quantity measuring duration." But throughout the rest of the book, I want you to think of time simply as 1,440 minutes. The purpose is to reel you in, to bring you present to the only time that matters, this moment **right now.** Do this and you will see how time becomes your best and most powerful friend quickly. So, no more 24 hours in a day, think 1440 slow minutes. It is an amazing feeling of more when you're in this zone of time! Your Time Awareness System™ (TAS) is now being activated; once that happens, it remains activated and can't be reversed. TAS works in unison with the Reticular Activating System, the part of the brain that lets you know whether something is important to you. Think of the RAS as the gatekeeper, sifting through the copious amounts of information that your brain daily encounters, trying to figure out which information is significant enough to let through and which should be pushed aside like junk-mail in your e-mail inbox. The mechanism is the same: if you don't assign some kind of filter to your e-mail system, you will be bombarded with useless junk every day, but if you take action to avoid this bombardment by deleting certain emails or designating them as the spam they are, you will be in control. In this way, once your TAS is activated, once the gatekeeper (RAS) puts time on high alert, time itself becomes a powerful force!

Once your brain accepts the declining 1440 minutes in a day concept for processing time, what you watch on television, the books and magazines you read, the movies you see, the number of innings you watch a baseball game, and the time you spend with others will all be processed by your brain in a different way.

**"Time discovers truth."** —Seneca

Do you realize that if you watched every baseball game played on TV in a year, you'd spend the time equivalent of more than two full years of college? That's right: 1 year = 162 games; 162 games at 3 hours per game x 60 minutes = 29,160 minutes.

*An associate's degree is equal to 25,200 minutes*
*(20 courses x 14 weeks x 90mins)*

Your ability to be present at the moment, instead of in the past or the future, keeps you in sync with the now, and being present in the moment ultimately creates the kind of future you want. Remember that the future is always a manifestation of how you're living currently, in the present. If you want to see what your future will look like, take a good, hard look at how you choose to use your daily minutes and compound them over the next six months!

**1440TIME**™ creates that slight sense of urgency or pressure that can be used as a motivational tool. It allows you to see a definite finish line to each day. By doing so, we intensify the perceived value of it—generating an internal scarcity, and when we have a scarcity of something—the price and or perceived value of it rises. Think about when you only have so much money in your pocket or purse, aren't you much more aware of what you will spend it on. The lack or scarcity of it has you much more in tune with what is important and what is not. Remember time and money has an inseparable connection in the world as we know it today for most. For now realize the old clock, *being separated by two twelve hour intervals*, was and is still today, used as a control mechanism to have you on automatic pilot, a "living zombie".

**"All things are difficult before they are easy."**
—Thomas Fuller

The book has been formulated to help free you from the archaic clock once and for all, and as quickly as possible. The amazing thing is, once these simple concepts from this book sink in, time will actually seem to slow—you will feel more in control of it—and time-related stress will diminish greatly. You will be able to do more in one day—or less on any given day, should you so choose than you ever thought possible. Let's take a look at this following formula:

$$(dm) \times (fa) = \textbf{EG}$$
daily minutes x focused action = **Exponential Growth**

Using this formula, we can determine how quickly we want the *result* to happen, just by the minutes and focused action we put into it. I call it the 'Real Rate of Return' on your 'TIME', and eventually you'll learn the fastest way to the completion of any goal, will be **"POWER-TIME PLUS"**. This is covered in more detail in The 1440 Power System® eBook. Visit www.1440time.com for more.

Think about all the times when you were forced to use your minutes in a certain way, such as when you had to reach a deadline for a project, or you overslept and had to catch a plane to get somewhere! What happened in most cases? That's right: you got it done. You found a way to make it happen. If you did not, or the results were less than expected, it was either because you hadn't put in the required daily minutes, or there was a lack of focused action. Time always has a way of becoming your friend when you need it the most.

**"A man of knowledge lives by acting, not by thinking about acting."** —Carlos Castaneda

Let us say you want to learn Spanish. The class is fourteen weeks, twice a week and sixty minutes long at the local college that equals 1,680 total minutes and 98 total days, but instead, you buy Rosetta Stone, and decide to teach yourself at home and even while commuting on the train. The formula for the above equation would look like this 20 x fa= 84, or 20 daily minutes of *focused action* will get you through the class in 84 days (20 x 84) = 1,680. Fourteen days sooner and less money spent.

**Double the minutes** to forty a day and you're done in forty-two days, what a concept!

Imagine what you can do when you apply this formula to any goal you want to complete. Remember the key to completing any goal you desire is to have a **start-date** and a **finish-line** attached to it. How much more efficient would you work if your boss said to you, "*this is what I need you to get done today, and if you get done early you can leave with full pay.*"Anything you want to get done just attach a timeline to it, and the daily minutes (*applying the power of compounding*) x focused action, and results not reasons will have you smiling.

Some of my readers might think this idea of time is crazy. But look at how the herd viewed Christopher Columbus in the 1400s when he insisted that the world was round. So, stop thinking of time in terms of twenty-four hours, a twelve-hour clock, and seven days in a week. Instead, think of a day in terms of 1440 minutes and see the world for what it is—round!

**"Following the light of the sun, we left the Old World."** —Christopher Columbus

The old way of thinking about clock time, which has been passed down from generation to generation, embodies the inherent error of our times today. Are we still using a dial-up connection today to get on the internet, a computer with 64Kb of RAM or a rotary phone? Think about it? Are we still using the telegraph, the horse, or the train to get information today, I don't think so? Why hasn't the way we process *time* progressed along with the speed of technology today? Is it not possible, since we are still using a time system from thousands of years ago—when information took days, weeks, months, and even years to be delivered, and the amount of information available was minuscule compared to what the brain has to process today—that our calibration with the ancient *chron*ological mechanical clock is off in the twenty-first century? Hence, why so many feel the pressure of time and have time-related stress and *chron*ic ailments? Why so many people seem to be in slow motion at work, home, and while in the grocery store? The truth is you can't find time in that old standard clock anymore. Its out-of-date speed is too slow for the modern world. But you have been taught this truth forever, so it has never occurred to you that standard archaic clock and calendar are out of tune! Therefore, it seems we're always chasing and stressing over time, as we suffer from Times Fault Syndrome (TFS) subconsciously, as the years just keep moving faster and faster by!

Thinking in terms of hours and using the standard clock in the days of Bonnie and Clyde was fine, but for today's hyperspeed, I don't think so. Might the minute countdown clock just be the natural progression in our human experience unrecognized?

**"The most damaging phrase in the language is: It's always been done that way."**
—Grace Hopper

# GET MOVING USING THE 1440 POWER SYSTEM® AND RECOGNIZE THE SIGNS OF THE TIMES.

So, what actually is the 1440 Power System® then? The 1440 Power System® is the connector to 1440TIME™. It breaks down those minutes further into three zones of time of a day, which are:

- **Sleep**
- **Work**
- **Free time (off, down, spare)**

In chapter sixteen when you'll learn more about the 1440 Power System®— the zones are changed to:

1. Sleep
2. Livelihood
3. On-Time

For now, realize that it is minutes over hours, and 1440 minutes over twenty-four hours in a day and you'll be fine.

Let's get back to work…

We have wasted so much of our daily time over the past ten years with sports time, TV time, movie time, drama time, play time, and stress time. We have burned and continue to burn time—while the consumers consume, and Wall Street is rich once again, as the Dow cracks through 22,000 as of this writing! Does Wall Street really care who won the Stanley Cup final; or that the Warriors got revenge on Lebron? That's right NO!!: they only care if they're making money *off the story*, by selling ad time to the TV, radio stations, newspapers, and magazines.

Have fun with your sports as fans, but realize if you're not in that business you make no money, but you spend it! You make time for it, but don't get paid for it, and your emotions ride in out like the daily tides, leaving you drained for your own victories for your game, **the game of life, that is.**

So many people I know live and die by their team winning or los-ing. The emotional energy used up whether their team wins or loses is immense. They could be drained for days. When their team wins, they're happier, they smile a lot, buy drinks for people, and work the next day is good, as enthusiasm reigns. When their team loses all bets are off, they're angry, upset, moody, stingy, and work the next day sucks, and this could last the entire week if it's their football team that lost.

I love sports as much as anyone, but do we have to watch and think about it that much? Is our life that boring that we have to find passion and thrill watching someone else's? So, no more excuses! No more blame! The world of time has no favorites—cares about no eth-nicity, age, or gender. We all have the same 1,440 minutes per day, and **what you do with them defines your future.**

Enjoy the game but maybe between innings get on your stationary bike for five minutes.

**Life is like a taxi. The meter just keeps a-ticking whether you are getting somewhere or just standing still."** —Lou Erickson

# LOOK AT SOME OF THE CLASSIC BLAMING OF TIME EXCUSES:

- "If I weren't so busy with the kids, I'd…"
- "If I only had the time, I'd…go to the gym, cook more, relax more, have more fun…"
- "If I'd had the time, I could have worked it out with my ex-wife (or ex-husband)…or my best friend…"

*Sounds like the Scarecrow: "If I only had a brain"*

Let me be clear. This is not about micromanaging time. Once a friend said to me, "Kevin, I can't micromanage my time the way you're suggesting. Accounting for every single minute is just way too much for my brain to handle." Well like the Scarecrow from the Wizard of Oz, we all have a large computer between our ears, and thinking regarding minutes is easy for our brain, so blame thyself not thy brain. Moreover, I believe most of our brains are the same for the masses, the difference being only the time spent studying, reading and learning about those particular studies that make the difference in knowledge known. Instead of telling time start measuring time. "And Oz never gave nothing to the Tin Man, that he didn't already have".

We all have **"EOT"…** Equal Opportunity Time…

**"The sum of the square roots of any two sides of an isosceles triangle is equal to the square root of the remaining side."**
—The Scarecrow from the Wizard of Oz

This is not about being obsessively analytical about time. Rather it is about being aware of time, how we use it, and ultimately to take **ownership** and full **responsibility** for its use.

Once we admit that it isn't time's fault, or our brains fault, or our parents fault, or the governments fault, or Wall Street's fault that keeps us from what we want to accomplish, we are forced to look within and confront the hard reality: the only thing that keeps us from accomplishing a goal usually is, **"we don't want it bad enough"**! The "time" has always been there.

*Admittance is the first step to recovery.*

Remember, this book doesn't tell you what to do or how to do it—it's just making it quite clear that **you have the time to do it, become it, attain it, or learn** about whatever it is that you really want to learn. Those who fail to adapt to the speed of change will be left behind. The world owes us nothing. But for those who want to succeed, there is only one secret…Time is your best friend and is plentiful!

**TIME T**hings **I M**ust **E**arn

On the next page, you will see a Time Conversion Table and some examples of time usage. It converts hours into minutes, think of it as adding more RAM to your human computer.

**"And in the end, it's not the years in your life that count. It's the life in your years."**
—Abraham Lincoln

## TIME CONVERSION TABLE

### The 1440 Power System®

- 1 year =         525,600         minutes
- 1 Quarter =     133,920         minutes
- 1 month =       44,640           minutes
- 1 week =         10,080           minutes
- 1 day=           1,440             minutes
- 1 hour =         60                 minutes

Take a good look at this table; take a picture of it on your phone, keep it accessible and remember it. It will help you on your path to "Time Mastery".

**"The unexamined life is not worth living"**
—Socrates

## SOME TIME USAGE STATISTICS

- ✓ **Free minutes in one year in a <u>normal work</u> week = 2,100 after:**
  - ° **Sleep seven hours**
  - ° **Work ten hours**
    - - **Free minutes seven hours (420 x 5 = 2,100)**

- ✓ **Free minutes on <u>weekends</u> for most = 1,920**
  - ° **Sleep eight hours**
    - - **Waking hours: sixteen (16 x 2 = 1,920)**

$$\underline{2,100 + 1,920(52)} = \mathbf{209,000}$$

Total free minutes for a typical person in one year equals 209,000, or 145 days. To put that in perspective the three events combined below equal about 100,000 minutes!

- • **A major league baseball season** *(150 minutes a game)*
- • **833 reruns of the Seinfeld show** *(30 minutes a show)*
- • **A four-year bachelor's degree** *(40 courses @ 14 weeks @ 90 minutes a class)*

Now multiply that by five years and you have over **one million minutes**! Let's be honest, if we had that time back would we use it differently this time? I bet we would appreciate it more for one thing. The fact is, we can't get that time back, but we can use it to learn from now on!

**If you want the present to be different from the past, study the past.** —Baruch Spinoza

# 11. IT'S THE MINUTES, NOT THE HOURS, THAT MAKE THE DIFFERENCE

I have to laugh when I bring up the Minute Clock or The 1440 Power System® with people I know and don't know. They usually pause and get a peculiar look on their face, then nod and smile politely, or simply agree, but I can see that they don't fully understand what I'm saying and are not ready for this awareness just yet. On the other hand, all I have to do is talk to them about morning minutes and their faces light up. They get it! Suddenly they understand what I'm trying to say. They know exactly how important every minute is in the morning, when they're trying to get the kids off to school, grab a cup of coffee, and get to work. *In the morning, it's the minutes—not the hours that count.* Oversleep by just ten minutes and the family's whole schedule can be thrown into chaos. No breakfast or coffee for you, Pop-tarts for the kids, a rush to beat the traffic—what a nightmare. The instant pressure of assuming you'll be late for work causes your stress to elevate even before you've climbed out of bed and headed for the shower. And did you know that according to our biological clock, (circadian rhythm), our blood pressure naturally has its sharpest rise around 6:45 A.M.? Isn't that a sure sign that the absolute worst time of day to be freaking out over time is in the early morning, exactly when most people are doing just that!

You're already using the minute clock in the morning; 1440TIME™ is just used all day and every day of the week. Let's say you know that mornings present a challenge. So instead of setting your alarm for 6:00am, you set it for 5:45am. This way you can have a whole fifteen extra minutes to sit and read the paper, or take a longer shower, or get the kids' lunches ready. Fifteen minutes to catch up on your to-do list, or jump on the treadmill. Fifteen minutes to de-stress your body, whatever. The day starts feeling in control, feeling good…the way it should.

*"People who feel that they are running out of time have sped up their biological clocks. They have faster heart rates and jittery platelets with high levels of adrenaline. When they drop dead from a premature heart attack, they have literally run out of time."*— *Deepak Chopra*

For most of us, the default program is to think in terms of hours, (snail mail) which are just too slow for an impatient society in a *now faster world*. Think of the difference it would make if you started to think in minutes instead. It's just more…Think of all those precious minutes you would have in the morning. Your daily morning time-stress would vanish, in turn leading to a pleasant commute, a happier work attitude, a more enjoyable sixty-minute lunch, and even the drive home would become a much healthier state of mind. *When you control the clock you can control the game.*

The **key** then to the 1440 Power System® is the ability to apply the same importance to the minutes we have in the morning to the minutes we have all day—whether they're Livelihood Minutes, Sleep Minutes or On-Time (free) Minutes.

**Look at the two clocks.**

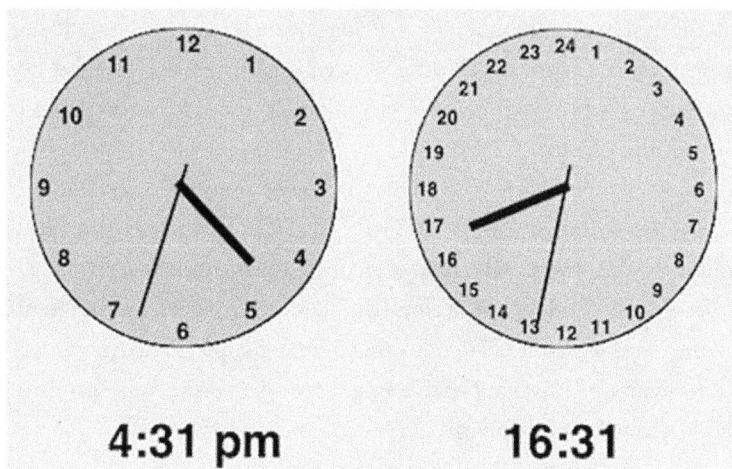

4:31 pm          16:31

* http://24hourtime.info/the-24-hour-time-system/

Go to the web address above and then scroll down and click on the link to the YouTube video showing the two clocks. The video compares a typical twelve-hour clock with a twenty-four-hour clock. Hit the play button and you will see the two clocks run side by side. You'll probably note the interesting effect that the twenty-four-hour clock appears to have more time in the day, and the twelve-hour clock is moving faster than the twenty-four-hour clock. The old standard clock uses overlapping numbers was fine for back in 45BC. It makes time *chronological*, *static*, a list of events arranged in sequences of time, much like a train schedule, same times every day, like us: we get up at 6:00am, work by 8:00, break at 10:00, lunch at noon, break at 3:00, works over at 5:00, dinner by 6:00, take the kid to dance by 7:00, the game or show starts at 8:00, pickup kid at 9:00, get in bed by 10:00, watch some TV until 11:00 and be sleeping by 11:30. Meet Chronos, the god of linear and orderly time. Some call it Groundhogs day?

The U.S. military understands how this works: not only does it cause less confusion in the accuracy of time throughout the world, but the twenty-four-hour clock helps measure one full day. It has a larger picture of how much time you really have in a day, and the clock becomes a tool for exponential productivity gains. Time becomes the ally, not the enemy.

I hope to introduce 1440TIME™ to S&P companies and the US Military—the most effective real-time measurement system ever devised. Transcending linear clock time, unlocking even more potential and urgency, which is needed for this ever faster-paced do more world, just to keep up? Anything that is important is measured in some way! Think about it? But time, the greatest commodity of all time is not!? We call it a clock and it tells you what time it is!

Finally, I want to give thanks to my Dad, Robert L. McGrane. A Marine who served his country; awarded three Purple Hearts in the Korean War, loved his wife Patricia and children, and man who said it like this **"I might have strong opinions, but I never judge"**. Robert spoke very few words, but when he did, you knew it. My Dad just passed on today as of this writing, July 23, 2014(4:45pm). We all love you Dad; we're going to miss you and say hello to Mom for us… We love you!!!

And let us not forget all who are serving, served and who have passed on protecting this great nation, allowing us to live our *time* **free and safer**.

**"The  person who opposes having the results measured accurately already knows that the results are inadequate.  "**—Anonymous

The two clocks below are both based on twenty-four-hour days; one is the twelve-hour clock we currently use while the other is the twenty-four-hour clock the military uses. Assuming a cycle in which the average person spends six hours a day sleeping (360 minutes), we'll block out the period of 12:00am to 6:00am on both clocks.

**Twelve-Hour Clock        Twenty-Four-Hour Clock**

What I find is that the twenty-four-hour clock appears to have more time in a day, even though the same number of hours has been blocked out. In reality, there is no difference. But isn't reality based on our perception? And even though both clocks control, one relies on conformity and limitations, while the other is based opportunity, learning, success, and victory.

**"Reality in our century is not something to be faced."** —Graham Greene

The 1440TIME™ countdown clock helps us see and feel, how much waking time we really have in a day. Simply by virtue of a changed visual perception, we can start to think about our world differently. If we *perceive* that we have more time in a day, we will *have* more time in a day. Only our lack of imagination is an excuse for not having enough. That's why the old twelve-hour standard clock and calendar protocol is not an efficient time system anymore. It may work for social conditioning, get people to work, or an appointment on time, but it masks the true spirit of time, and does very little for enhancement of *personal productivity*. You have 1440 minutes every day and about one thousand out of bed. Surely, you can find the time for most anything when you break them into minutes like this.

Try it out for yourself and then say it doesn't work. Go to www.1440time.com

**"I must govern the clock, not be governed by it."** —Golda Meir

# 12. THE CLOCKS OF LIFE

*Perception or Reality?*

### "Is it Live or is it Memorex?"®

Who remembers that Memorex® commercial from the '80s? Were you like me, never knowing which was which?

Our perception of time can be faster or slower. If we are able to create this effect simply by changing the way we think about time, why not slow it down and have more of it? Or, if we're somewhere we would rather not be, (*e.g. the DMV or traffic court*) be able to change the perception to make it go faster?

We have the power to choose how we process time, and even to slow it down, or speed it up—but no power to get it back once it is gone!

Perception is reality. Whatever we focus on expands. The child focuses on how long an hour is, while an older person focuses on how fast it goes by. Focusing on the length of time expands that length even more, while focusing on how fast it is going by speeds it up even more. All an illusion, but the effects are real!

For most reading this book, you already know how to keep your mind busy while waiting at the doctor's office which *speeds up time*, but the real Holy Grail is, how to *slow down the clock of our lives*!

**"All that we are is the result of what we have thought. The mind is everything. What we think, we become."** —Maharishi Mahesh Yogi

Look at the **two Life Clocks**. Both are Bertrand Planes creations, each serving a different purpose. **Life Clock A** is based on a life expectancy to eighty-four. **Life Clock B** is the illusion of how time feels—the years seem to go steadily faster as we age.

(Source: http://www.bertrandplanes.com).

A                                    B

But we all know that logically time has always been the same: 24 hours per day—whether at seven, fourteen, twenty-eight, forty-two, seventy, or seventy-seven years of age. Bertrand Planes' illustration may be only a visual representation of how time seems to move more quickly as we get older, but if we believe the illusion and most do, our minds and hearts will go along for the ride. Throw in some social proof from others, and you now have the validation needed! **Time, in fact gets faster and faster as we get older.** What if we knew why this illusion seems and feels real and can do something to change it?

**"The passage of time is simply an illusion created by our brains." **—A.M.W. Ball

As members of a society in which *time is palpable, time is of the essence, time plays on our looks, time takes a toll on our bodies, it's only a matter of time, but time is kinder to those who grasp it, and even more so to those who respect it, and truly value it...*

With our biological clocks always ticking into the future, is there any way we can shift our perspective and experience to see time in a new way that just might slow it down. Yes, by appreciating *time* the way an eighty-year-old person does and process time like the eight-year-old child does. *Think and ponder about that for a second or two?*

A client stopped by my office 3:00 pm on June 1$^{st}$ to ask me a few questions about the economy. "Kevin," he said, "can you believe how fast this year is flying by? It'll be the Fourth of July soon. Before you know it September will be here!" "Slow down, Rich," I said, motioning for him to have a seat and relax. "We still have over thirty days left in the second quarter of the year, and then it's another ninety days before September will be here. Did you know that's over 133,000 minutes and we still have over 540 minutes left today before we go to sleep."

Have it any way you want, be like Rich or be like Kevin... It's your call.

Rich is still looking at time from an outdated clock and calendar perspective (linear).

**"Only a person who lives not in time but in the present is happy"** —Ludwig Wittgenstein

## S L O W I N G IT DOWN

With conscious intent, I have learned to slow down time by chang-ing the perception of the clock and calendar. That's right. I now live a life in which the days, weeks, months, and years have slowed down dra-matically. How did I do it? First, I shifted to 1440TIME™ and utilize the 1440 Power System® daily. Second, I use the 365togo calendar, more on this in chapter 18. Both do the same thing, they slow down time. One slows down the day, the other, the week, month, quarter, and year. The 1440 Power System® and the 365togo calendar both leverage time, by chunking or breaking it down into smaller units.

> *"A simple but effective principle used in some creative methods*
> *and problem-solving approaches is to break down the situation*
> *or item under scrutiny into its component parts."*
> —CreatingMinds.org

## BREAKING IT DOWN

Breaking things down into smaller components is a strategy that many business professionals, teachers, and coaches, whether for training purposes or to learn something with less stress and more efficiency. In terms of time, this process works perfectly for breaking down the calendar and clock to achieve the results we want, that is to slow the clock of life down, and to reach the goals we set forth for ourselves! *This method works best for people who have defined goals and set timelines to finish tasks.*

**"Nothing is particularly hard, if you divide it into small jobs."** —Ray Kroc

## HOW IT WORKS

The next few pages are all about breaking down the yearly calendar from the one-year increment on which it is based to its smallest component—the 1,440 minutes of each day that make up the 365 days (525,600 minutes) of the year.

1. Yearly calendar
2. Quarterly view
3. Monthly look
4. Weekly perspective
5. The Daily Time-Voucher. The 1440 minutes we have each day.

The more anchored and mindful we are in the **right now's** of our lives, the slower time moves.

---

### DAILY TIME-VOUCHER

#### Worth <u>1440</u> Minutes

#### Good for Today Only!!!!

---

**"Time is free, but it's priceless. You can't own it, but you can use it. You can't keep it, but you can spend it. Once you've lost it you can never get it back."** —Harvey McKay Quotes

We'll start by focusing on the **first quarter—January, February, March**—but we'll do that knowing we have the entire year as a backdrop. These calendars are being used for visual concept only.

## 2014

### January

| Su | Mo | Tu | We | Th | Fr | Sa |
|----|----|----|----|----|----|----|
|    |    |    | 1  | 2  | 3  | 4  |
| 5  | 6  | 7  | 8  | 9  | 10 | 11 |
| 12 | 13 | 14 | 15 | 16 | 17 | 18 |
| 19 | 20 | 21 | 22 | 23 | 24 | 25 |
| 26 | 27 | 28 | 29 | 30 | 31 |    |

### February

| Su | Mo | Tu | We | Th | Fr | Sa |
|----|----|----|----|----|----|----|
|    |    |    |    |    | 1  | 2  |
| 3  | 4  | 5  | 6  | 7  | 8  | 9  |
| 10 | 11 | 12 | 13 | 14 | 15 | 16 |
| 17 | 18 | 19 | 20 | 21 | 22 | 23 |
| 24 | 25 | 26 | 27 | 28 |    |    |

### March

| Su | Mo | Tu | We | Th | Fr | Sa |
|----|----|----|----|----|----|----|
|    |    |    |    |    |    | 1  |
| 2  | 3  | 4  | 5  | 6  | 7  | 8  |
| 9  | 10 | 11 | 12 | 13 | 14 | 15 |
| 16 | 17 | 18 | 19 | 20 | 21 | 22 |
| 23 | 24 | 25 | 26 | 27 | 28 | 29 |
| 30 | 31 |    |    |    |    |    |

### April

| Su | Mo | Tu | We | Th | Fr | Sa |
|----|----|----|----|----|----|----|
|    |    | 1  | 2  | 3  | 4  | 5  |
| 6  | 7  | 8  | 9  | 10 | 11 | 12 |
| 13 | 14 | 15 | 16 | 17 | 18 | 19 |
| 20 | 21 | 22 | 23 | 24 | 25 | 26 |
| 27 | 28 | 29 | 30 |    |    |    |

### May

| Su | Mo | Tu | We | Th | Fr | Sa |
|----|----|----|----|----|----|----|
|    |    |    |    | 1  | 2  | 3  |
| 4  | 5  | 6  | 7  | 8  | 9  | 10 |
| 11 | 12 | 13 | 14 | 15 | 16 | 17 |
| 18 | 19 | 20 | 21 | 22 | 23 | 24 |
| 25 | 26 | 27 | 28 | 29 | 30 | 31 |

### June

| Su | Mo | Tu | We | Th | Fr | Sa |
|----|----|----|----|----|----|----|
| 1  | 2  | 3  | 4  | 5  | 6  | 7  |
| 8  | 9  | 10 | 11 | 12 | 13 | 14 |
| 15 | 16 | 17 | 18 | 19 | 20 | 21 |
| 22 | 23 | 24 | 25 | 26 | 27 | 28 |
| 29 | 30 |    |    |    |    |    |

### July

| Su | Mo | Tu | We | Th | Fr | Sa |
|----|----|----|----|----|----|----|
|    |    | 1  | 2  | 3  | 4  | 5  |
| 6  | 7  | 8  | 9  | 10 | 11 | 12 |
| 13 | 14 | 15 | 16 | 17 | 18 | 19 |
| 20 | 21 | 22 | 23 | 24 | 25 | 26 |
| 27 | 28 | 29 | 30 | 31 |    |    |

### August

| Su | Mo | Tu | We | Th | Fr | Sa |
|----|----|----|----|----|----|----|
|    |    |    |    |    | 1  | 2  |
| 3  | 4  | 5  | 6  | 7  | 8  | 9  |
| 10 | 11 | 12 | 13 | 14 | 15 | 16 |
| 17 | 18 | 19 | 20 | 21 | 22 | 23 |
| 24 | 25 | 26 | 27 | 28 | 29 | 30 |
| 31 |    |    |    |    |    |    |

### September

| Su | Mo | Tu | We | Th | Fr | Sa |
|----|----|----|----|----|----|----|
|    | 1  | 2  | 3  | 4  | 5  | 6  |
| 7  | 8  | 9  | 10 | 11 | 12 | 13 |
| 14 | 15 | 16 | 17 | 18 | 19 | 20 |
| 21 | 22 | 23 | 24 | 25 | 26 | 27 |
| 28 | 29 | 30 |    |    |    |    |

### October

| Su | Mo | Tu | We | Th | Fr | Sa |
|----|----|----|----|----|----|----|
|    |    |    | 1  | 2  | 3  | 4  |
| 5  | 6  | 7  | 8  | 9  | 10 | 11 |
| 12 | 13 | 14 | 15 | 16 | 17 | 18 |
| 19 | 20 | 21 | 22 | 23 | 24 | 25 |
| 26 | 27 | 28 | 29 | 30 | 31 |    |

### November

| Su | Mo | Tu | We | Th | Fr | Sa |
|----|----|----|----|----|----|----|
|    |    |    |    |    |    | 1  |
| 2  | 3  | 4  | 5  | 6  | 7  | 8  |
| 9  | 10 | 11 | 12 | 13 | 14 | 15 |
| 16 | 17 | 18 | 19 | 20 | 21 | 22 |
| 23 | 24 | 25 | 26 | 27 | 28 | 29 |
| 30 |    |    |    |    |    |    |

### December

| Su | Mo | Tu | We | Th | Fr | Sa |
|----|----|----|----|----|----|----|
|    | 1  | 2  | 3  | 4  | 5  | 6  |
| 7  | 8  | 9  | 10 | 11 | 12 | 13 |
| 14 | 15 | 16 | 17 | 18 | 19 | 20 |
| 21 | 22 | 23 | 24 | 25 | 26 | 27 |
| 28 | 29 | 30 | 31 |    |    |    |

**Calendar from printfree.com**

**"The day is of infinite length for him who knows how to appreciate and use it."**
—J W Goethe

Next, break the quarter down to the current month **January**— yet keeping a watchful eye on the quarter.

| January 2014 | | | | | | |
|---|---|---|---|---|---|---|
| Sunday | Monday | Tuesday | Wednesday | Thursday | Friday | Saturday |
| | | | 1 | 2 | 3 | 4 |
| 5 | 6 | 7 | 8 | 9 | 10 | 11 |
| 12 | 13 | 14 | 15 | 16 | 17 | 18 |
| 19 | 20 | 21 | 22 | 23 | 24 | 25 |
| 26 | 27 | 28 | 29 | 30 | 31 | |

| February 2014 | | | | | | |
|---|---|---|---|---|---|---|
| | | | | | | 1 |
| 2 | 3 | 4 | 5 | 6 | 7 | 8 |
| 9 | 10 | 11 | 12 | 13 | 14 | 15 |
| 16 | 17 | 18 | 19 | 20 | 21 | 22 |
| 23 | 24 | 25 | 26 | 27 | 28 | |

| March 2014 | | | | | | |
|---|---|---|---|---|---|---|
| | | | | | | 1 |
| 2 | 3 | 4 | 5 | 6 | 7 | 8 |
| 9 | 10 | 11 | 12 | 13 | 14 | 15 |
| 16 | 17 | 18 | 19 | 20 | 21 | 22 |
| 23 | 24 | 25 | 26 | 27 | 28 | 29 |
| 30 | 31 | | | | | |

Calendar from printfree.com

**"Calendars are for careful people, not passionate ones."** —Chuck Sigars

## NEXT, THE CURRENT MONTH

| January 2014 | | | | | | |
|---|---|---|---|---|---|---|
| **Sunday** | **Monday** | **Tuesday** | **Wednesday** | **Thursday** | **Friday** | **Saturday** |
| | | | 1 | 2 | 3 | 4 |
| 5 | 6 | 7 | 8 | 9 | 10 | 11 |
| 12 | 13 | 14 | 15 | 16 | 17 | 18 |
| 19 | 20 | 21 | 22 | 23 | 24 | 25 |
| 26 | 27 | 28 | 29 | 30 | 31 | |

Looking at the calendar this way, we're taking the full year and breaking it down into smaller chunks (quarters and months). Remember it's your quarters that make your year, your months that make your quarters, your weeks that make your months, your days that make your weeks, and your minutes that make your days, which ultimately lead to the completion of your goals sometime in the future. This is just another tool in the overall time transformation that you are adjusting to now.

**"You tell me, and I forget. You teach me, and I remember. You involve me, and I learn."**
—Benjamin Franklin

Now it is time to break the month into one week:

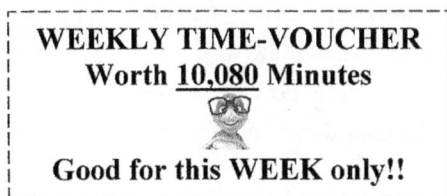

```
WEEKLY TIME-VOUCHER
Worth 10,080 Minutes

Good for this WEEK only!!
```

**Monday thru Sunday**

| Monday | Work! The plan or goal | Saturday & |
|---|---|---|
| Start plan or goal | here, using a little piece of your time-voucher daily. | Sunday Review & monitor |

Finally, now to your 1,440 minutes:

```
DAILY TIME-VOUCHER
Worth 1440 Minutes

Good for Today Only!!!!
```

**"A goal is a dream with a deadline."**
—Napoleon Hill

Let's look at an example of how this works. A championship billiard professional concentrates intensely on the shot at hand as she's walking around the table, planning her next series of shots. The table becomes the canvas of her mind as she strategizes her plays. Having this clear picture of exactly how she will run the table out before it's done, gives her the confidence and focused action **to do it**.

We can do the same thing with time! Start with the current shot: 1440TIME™ and the 1440 Power System®. Then look ahead to the week, month, quarter, and year using the 365togo calendar format, as the canvas of your mind to strategize your plays out—i.e., vision, goals, dreams, passions. I call this putting time into chunks—breaking it down into a series of shorter, attainable goals—now giving you that clear picture of exactly how you will run the year out, which in turn gives you the confidence and perspective that it can and will be done.

This process utilizes two-thirds of our Trilogy of Time—the **1440 Power System®** and the **Compound Value of Time**. We set forth our goals one day or one week at a time using one of these formulas: dm x fa= ER (daily minutes x focused action = Exponential Results), or wm x fa= ER (weekly minutes x focused action = Exponential Results). *Remember just 20 minutes a day is equal to three full-time college courses in one year.* The catch is to utilize the <u>power of compounding small units' of time over lots of time.</u> Sounds easy and is, but do you have the discipline to do it?

**"I long to accomplish a great and noble task, but it is my chief duty to accomplish small tasks as if they were great and noble."**
—Helen Keller

## PERSONAL PRODUCTIVITY ENHANCEMENT

Since this is a personal productivity enhancement book first and foremost, let's talk about how you can improve your productivity right now by using the On-Time Voucher provided below.

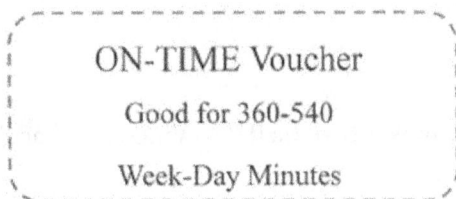

ON-TIME Voucher

Good for 360-540

Week-Day Minutes

Suddenly time becomes organized and available; here it is— here you go. OT has you moving forward now, permanently expanding your sense of time, as a surge of motivation fills your being. *Time's Fault Syndrome (TFS), has ultimately been destroyed!*

Twenty to sixty minutes of your OT voucher are to be used *exclusively* for things like self-education and physical fitness. And writing down thoughts and ideas for the completion of any task or goal. Use them wisely and **write down** the things you need to get done somewhere. We'll talk more about this tool in upcoming chapters, but for now remember, it's the minutes that create your future, the minutes that give you more, and it's the minutes that slow down the clock of your mind.

**"No matter how busy you may think you are, you must find time for reading, or surrender yourself to self-chosen ignorance."**
—Confucius

# 13. OWNERSHIP OF UNDER-STANDING IS MOTIVATION IN ITSELF

**"Men, this is a football."** —Vince Lombardi

As simple as that quote sounds, everything starts with the execution of the basic building blocks. Vince Lombardi, one of the greatest football coaches of all time, knew this. He broke the game down to its simplest components, perfected the basics, and had a clear vision of the outcome—to win the game. As your Life-Time coach, I say to you, "friends, this is time"—the core building block of the game of life. It's what we all get to use every day: no one has any more or any less. What makes us different as individuals are how we use this most basic of all building blocks, *time itself*... It is rarely anything else that makes the difference in success or failure. For many people, the time has become the excuse, the hidden enemy, instead of a teammate. It doesn't have to be that way. Looking at time as the finest playmaker in your arsenal is the first step to time mastery and ultimately to transcend linear time.

Time as the crutch in the blame game of life, or time as the tool for results and purpose—it is your choice, the blue or the red pill?

## LET'S RECAP:

1. We get only a one-time-ticket into the great game of life, and that ticket is activated at birth.

2. There are 1440 minutes in one day, which are equal to 24 hours, and we now think in terms of minutes only.

3. You know you have plenty of time in a year to set and complete your annual goals and even more, because there are 365 days and 525,600 minutes in one year, of which *145 days* or *200,000 minutes*, or about forty percent of those days and minutes are of free-time. That time available after subtracting out sleep and work, called **On-Time** minutes in the 1440 Power System®. The **difference maker** and where PowerTime Plus resides to make you a perianal all-star.

4. You realize the days of the week and the months of the year are just trance like words—and come from obsolete ancient mythologies and ideologies from the past. No longer having power over the way you feel about them. Time is just a series of sun rises *1,440 minutes* long, (*the content*) counting down until your one-ticket on the Life-Clock (the *context*) runs out here in the natural on planet Earth. A Monday is no different than any other day in a week, 1440 is 1440!

5. You know if time is a tight during the work-week to build on those *goals you set*, it's okay…because you have over **2,000 weekend On-Time minutes** waiting for you to score those touchdowns in the red zone, and you do!

**"The clock we are not, the time we are."**
—Kevin McGrane

A few years ago, I met a man who was on his way home after a day of teaching. While we sat and had something to eat, we started talking about education and motivation. This man had traveled the world. Teaching was his calling and his passion; I could see it in his eyes and hear it in his words. The man said, **"Kevin, ownership of understanding is motivation in itself."** I interpret the man's words to mean that when you own it and understand it, you will be motivated to do it, apply it, use it, and teach it.

When you fully understand and experience 1440TIME™, you have to **own it**! You can't help but be motivated by it, apply it, use it, and even teach it! If not, you are just not ready yet.

You have 1,440 minutes in each day, of which at least 1,000 are waking minutes that can be used to get things done, make things happen, and live with purpose!

**"Wisdom is the power to put our time and our knowledge to the proper use."**
—Thomas J. Watson

Acknowledging time as our greatest gift makes everything better because you're coming from a place of genuine appreciation. Nevertheless, since time is **not tangible**, it's hard to see outside the structured clock and calendar we have been conditioned by over the centuries.

So many today lose sight of the now and let things, circumstances, and others take up parking space in their mind by talking and listening to the media daily, about what's going on in the country, your sports team or the *pop stars*. Burning up (consuming) way too much of their *On-Time* watching others (the producers) spending theirs... You're either a **consumer** of *time* or a **producer** of time. Many in this country are consumers of *time*. After they come home from their job, the clock consumes their On-Time! But on what? If we measured it, we would know it, wouldn't we?

In economics, the consumer makes up the majority of the economy, while the producers take the money you spend. So, we need the consumer to spend their money and more to keep the stock market going higher. The same way you spend your On-Time minutes watching a live event, your time is being 'consumed' by watching the 'producers' of time making the big cash. Again, nothing wrong with this, as long as you recognize the distinction 'consumer' or 'producer' of time, and take full ownership of it, all is perfect.

*Remember,* **ownership of understanding is motivation in itself**. *So, once we own it and understand it, we should be motivated to apply it and use it! Right?*

**"Time stays where it is, it is us that passes."**
—Zen Master Dojen

# 14. WHEN YOU CONTROL THE CLOCK, YOU CONTROL THE GAME

As I was watching a football game on Monday night, a team drove eighty yards down the field in sixteen plays, using nine minutes and thirteen seconds off of the first quarter's fifteen-minute time clock, when the commentator said, "When you control the clock, you control the game."

Professional football has many similarities to life in the natural. Both are games. Both get a fresh start every year. Both have time limits. Both have a form of parity: pro football has the salary cap, and life has a **time cap**, with the same constant fourteen hundred and forty minutes in each day **for all**. Both football and life need good clock management, and both need teamwork to be successful. Both need a formula and proper execution of that formula to be successful. Both show you what you can do when a sense of urgency and an active will is applied. Football needs to make plays to win, and in life, we have to make time to win. A field goal is good, but a touchdown in the red zone is better if looking to win in life, fifteen minutes a day working out or for self-education is good, but forty-five minutes or more is a touchdown.

*By the way, I heard the price of a thirty-second commercial for the 2016 Super Bowl was about $5 million. So it seems that when you control the clock, you control the money, too.*

The first step to taking control of the clock is to think in terms of **minutes** not hours, **zones** not names of days of a week, and the **365togo** calendar format. As this approach becomes the logical sequence of your mind, controlling the clock becomes easier, more automatic and providence soon takes over. Before a football game, the coach doesn't say, "Gentlemen, we have one hour to play our hearts out, let's go out there and do it!" He says, "Men, we have four quarters in this game, each being fifteen minutes long. Go out there and play each one like it was your last"! When we apply the same breakdown concept in our daily lives using The 1440 Power System® (i.e. Sleep, Livelihood, and OT), each zone of the day becomes the area you play and focus on, much like playing each quarter of a football game.

The standard clock is not *time*. Time is an **opportunity** and **being present**, (the playing field of life). The mechanical clock is a *robotic and a conditioning ruse* (a mere spectator, watching others play). You must step out of that clock time, call an audible and adapt to life's changing speed and make a play. You make the choice. A world without borders and boundaries where anything is possible or a world structured and controlled by numbers on a circular sphere, obsolete ancient gods for names of days, your sport teams, TV schedules, social networks, and or others.

The practice, the blackboard, the physical training, the season games, and the playoffs are **content** (the 1440 minutes we have each day). The Super Bowl is the **context**, the big picture (the life clock, only getting one ticket into this great game of life).

**"Winning isn't everything, but the will to win is everything."** —Vince Lombardi

## RETICULAR ACTIVATING SYSTEM

Taking control of your daily time clock and managing it activates the Reticular Activating System (RAS); remember the part of the brain that determines what is important and what is not—*the gatekeeper sifting through information that floods your brain every moment.* Whatever thoughts you repeat consistently become the program for the brain to process. So, catch yourself when you say things like, "I never have enough time", "I'm always late," "I have nothing to do" or "where did the weekend go." You have plenty of time, you're always on time, you have goals to meet, and your weekends are now turtle like.

Awareness is the key to being mindful, and the *1440 declining clock system* brings you there at a glance anytime and anywhere. There is no easier and efficient way to become present than seeing **how much time you have left on this date**, right on your phone or wrist. Much like the movie "In Time" with Justin Timberlake, the difference being you died when your time ran out. For us, it's only our goals and dreams that die or get delayed for another day.

Once your *Time Awareness System*™ *is activated*, time itself becomes the dominant force, and the gatekeeper puts **time on high alert**. You become a great time strategist, able to use your time efficiently and effectively throughout your day, just as a football coach must navigate the time clock or pay the consequences in the end.

**"Accusing the Times is but excusing ourselves."** —Thomas Fuller

# 15. DOES ANYBODY REALLY KNOW WHAT TIME IT IS?

*"As I s walking down the street one day, a man came up to me and asked me what the time was that was on my watch, and I said...Does anybody really know what time it is, does anybody really care....?"*

Who remembers this Chicago song from 1969? Even though I was only eight then, I was still affected by the music and the moments of that time.

The sixties were a time of technological advances, revolutions, social change, crazy fashion, rock and roll, civil rights, gay and women's liberation. We landed on the moon, had peace movements, the World's Fair, and the Vietnam War, where close to sixty thousand Americans and as many as two million Vietnamese lost their lives. Growing up in the '60s and '70s was amazing. Our neighborhood was loaded with kids and getting any type of game together was as easy as waking up in the morning. Which sport we played depended on what season it was? As long as we had a football, basketball, baseball, or hockey stick, we were good to go. And when we weren't playing sports, we were riding bikes. If we weren't riding, we were building tree forts or playing manhunt in the woods. We had few appliances, one TV, and a record player. The VCR was invented in 1971 but was rarely in the house enough to watch it. Life was fun from sunup to sundown and we all had plenty of time.

The speed of our lives has changed since those '60s and '70s—much the way the vinyl 33-rpm records have changed to WAV files. It is my view that instead of always fighting and vying for time with the old standard clock and calendar, we change our perception of the time altogether. But to do that we have to put down the old 33-rpm record player that we're still trying to use in a world of satellite radio, iPod's, and ipads, and flow with it, by implementing the 1440 Power System® and 1440TIME™ daily. Known as *measured time!*

Times change! Technology has changed! *We* change! And how we see *clock time should have changed*, because the old standard clock with us today is as obsolete as the reel-to-reel tape recorder. We must retire it immediately!

*"It is estimated that a week's worth of the* **New York Times** *contains more information than a person was likely to come across in a lifetime in the 18th century."* According to the "Did You Know" 3.0 video series

If everything is always changing and the speed of change is happening faster. Maybe a simple variation in the way we process time today is indeed in order. Our objective here is to cause a time awareness explosion, which starts with being aware and grateful for the one ticket we receive to get in this life, and second to be present and *absorbed in the now*. Unfortunately, easier said than done, in this fast past world—as stress—money—relationships, children, and health take their daily toll on the many—leaving them fighting, chasing and at odds with the clock, and therefore at odds with time itself.

**"Life belongs to the living and he who lives must be prepared for changes"**
—Johann Wolfgang von Goethe

This book was created to change the way you look and feel about time, to help build a deeper understanding of this most precious of all gifts. You get one daily Time-Voucher worth 1, 440 minutes, and it's in those moments that ultimately define our lives! We also only get one Life-Time ticket into the great park of life, so use it wisely. Remember you must not only "think outside the clock™," you have to do something with some of your "free" minutes daily. "Don't be just a consumer of time".

No one can exercise or read for you. No one can take the classes— or attend the webinars for you. There are shortcuts and quicker methods, but there is no free ticket into the park of success. You either choose to blame and hide behind the ancient clock and calendar or you just go-for-it or GTIME™ it by using 1440TIME™!

To steer you in the right direction, I'm starting each of my readers off with one GTIME™ Voucher. But it's good for today only, so enjoy it. This one is on me!

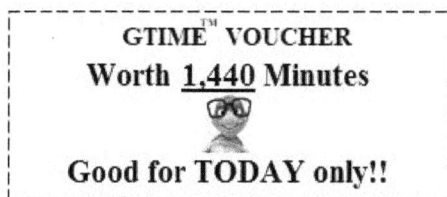

```
┌─────────────────────────────────────┐
│     GTIME™ VOUCHER                   │
│   Worth 1,440 Minutes                │
│         👓                           │
│                                      │
│   Good for TODAY only!!              │
└─────────────────────────────────────┘
```

**"Modern man thinks he loses something-- time--when he does not do things quickly. Yet he does not know what to do with the time he gains—except kill it."** —Erich Fromm

## IT'S TIME TO GET BACK TO WORK

Let's say you're at the batting range, where there are mechanical pitchers throwing balls at all different speeds—slow, medium, fast, and super-fast. You haven't hit a ball in years, and your timing is off. So what do you do? You can take one of two approaches to get your timing up to speed to be able to hit the fast pitch. Either (1) work up to the fast speed, going through the incremental stages from slow to medium and finally to fast, or (2) go directly to the super-fast and work your way back down to the fast speed. If you take the first approach, it will take longer but will work. Take the second method, and I bet that after seeing the super-fast pitch whiz by you several times, you'll be able to step down right into the fast cage and make contact with the ball.

A method taught in speed-reading uses the same approach, but instead of a super-fast pitch coming at you at 98mph, they send 10,000 words in twenty seconds at you, then 5,000, 2,500, 1000. By the time you get to 600 words a minute, it seems really slow, and 250 words a minute (*about what the average person can read*) is like watching paint dry. Speed-reading with a little practice easily doubles your words read per minute. It is a great tool for saving time, gaining quicker knowledge, and increases right brain activity.

The Emergency Medical Technician (EMT) at the scene of an unfortunate accident or the day trader who trades stocks every day. What do these professionals have in common? They both work inside the same clock. These individuals don't think in terms of days or hours; they exist inside the *minute clock*...in the *second clock, even milliseconds*! There are sixty seconds inside the minute clock. The EMT must get oxygen to the brain within 240 to 360 seconds (four to six minutes) and get the patient to the nearest hospital as fast as possible.

The day trader can make or lose a week's pay in less than sixty seconds. These professions calibrate at 78 RPMs as they work inside the minute clock because that's required for that type of work.

Do we have to live our lives inside the minute or second clock? No. But I am trying to get your brain processing speed (BPS) up to 45 rpm (minutes) and off the 33 RPM's (hours) of the 1960s. It's time to think inside the hour clock! Remember, you can do a lot more in **sixty minutes** than you can in one single hour.

Look at sports today? Are they still using the second clock? Or have they made the adjustment now, measuring at the millisecond, to see if the ball was out of the hand or not before the time went off!?

Go to: http://the1440powersystem.blogspot.com/2014/12/ step-one-calibrate-to-1440time.html!? to calibrate real-time.

**"Awareness without action is worthless."**
—Dr. Phil

# 16. WALL STREET GETS IT; MAIN STREET DOES NOT

We are still in the early framework of the Communication and Information age, with Wi-Fi, FiOS, hundreds of TV channels, streaming video, Facebook, Twitter, and smartphones delivering information and content at record speeds. Though this would seem like plenty, we still have a long way to go. Look at this tiny sample of future technology predictions, from futureforall.org:

**Computers that predict the future**

▷ **Computer mediators that resolve legal disputes**

▷ **Age reversal; extended/eternal life**

▷ **Human cloning**

▷ **Complete digital record of your life**

▷ **Mind/emotion control devices**

▷ **Brain enhancement implants**

▷ **Downloadable training experience (e.g., the ability to fly a jet or guide a submarine**

▷ Teleportation

▷ Time machines

▷ Flying boots

▷ Virtual/Augmented reality

▷ Language translator implants

▷ Telepathy

▷ Phone implants

▷ Mind-reading computers

▷ Deserts into forests

▷ Man-made precious materials like gold

▷ Ability to purify water instantly

▷ Underground cities.

Wow! And I thought high-speed Internet access and the Smartphone were the Holy Grail!

**"You only have control over three things in your life. The thoughts you think, the images you visualize, and the action you take**—Jack Canfield

The Smartphone, like the Internet, is widely used for the **consumption** of time and not the **production** of time, (e.g., talking, texting, entertainment, weather, directions). Meanwhile, Wall Street exploits these great tools, along with many other high technologies, leveraging their capabilities and taking productivity to the highest levels in history.

### It's Main Street's time to get with the program!

Our ability to receive information in seconds, twenty-four hours a day, has sped up the mind-chatter; unfortunately, this development has led us down a path of mental and physical laziness. Many aren't using technology to step up their game, as the forty-to-sixty crowd feels the pressure of time moving ever faster. Meanwhile, many kids have little understanding of the larger reality of our world today, as they subscribe to the plug-and-play world of thinking, adding additional psychological burden to their already overextended parents and teachers.

We are in the greatest of times as far as technological advancements, life expectancies, and amenities are concerned in this phenomenal internet age. A plethora of tools for knowledge and information are readily available—yet for the most part go unused (much like the hidden f's in that exercise from Chapter Three).

It's time to pair the two together: **1440TIME**™ and **Technology**.

**"In times of change, learners inherit the earth, while the learned find themselves beautifully equipped to deal with a world that no longer exists."** —Eric Hoffer

Our **personal** productivity in America I believe is at an all-time low for many, while business productivity is hitting highs. We hear this word "productivity" all the time on the financial news. Business productivity soars! Companies continue to increase their productivity as the NASDAQ is hitting all-time highs! If it works for Wall Street, then why not for Main Street? We have the same tech tools and capabilities available to us as Wall Street does!

## HERE ARE A FEW PRODUCTIVITY FACTORS:

- **Labor** is the amount of goods and services that a worker can produce in a given amount of time.
- **Technology** is the computer, microprocessor, fiber optics, smart phones, satellites, robotics, speed pass, etc.
- **Education** is the improved training that expands the skills of a worker, especially in the medical field. A few years ago, a medical student had specialized training in one skill set; now that same person has two, three, or more specific qualifications, enhancing productivity to save time and money for the medical facility.

Corporations not only know about productivity; they live it. Productivity is the reason for their ever-higher stock prices. Companies push productivity up and up while they continue to cut costs, lay off workers, and let high tech lead the way. This leaves millions on Main Street unemployed and waiting for things to turn around. Unfortunately, technological advancement is replacing people, too! It is what it is.

When Wall Street fires an employee, payroll taxes and health insurance premiums are reduced. Multiply the taxes and premiums by millions, and you can see the cost savings for these companies. Now add in technology, and you have a recipe for rising stock prices and wealth creation!

Being self-employed, I understand how technology increases productivity. Without it, I would need two other accountants, several more administrative assistants, and more materials during each tax season. So, what's the difference between business and personal productivity? If it's working for Wall Street, why not for Main Street?

**Main Street has taken the use of free time as far as it can. The time is now to transcend time, unleash its power, acknowledge it for what it is, and ignite personal productivity nationwide.** "But Kevin, I am doing hard physical work five days a week. I even work some weekends and the people on Wall St. are crooks and don't care about us!" I understand that more than you may think. As of this writing, I am working as "production" painter; painting big new homes eight hours a day (480 minutes) while on weekends I bartended and wait tables, all productivity-based jobs. Everyone has a task, and everyone works by the minute. Few were happy, the supervisors stressed out, and even I started to lose it after months of the nitpicking about the work. It was never fast enough, or good enough. "Time is money" as they said repeatedly. What is interesting though is what if they worked as hard on their personal life, as they did on their job? What a concept... I guess the "time is money" doesn't apply with their own time, huh...?

So, what is wrong with this picture? It seems we have no problem working hard for money for someone else, but when it comes to our own personal "free" time, we take the foot off the pedal. That is so odd! Or is it? After all, we are off the clock, and it's free-time!

It's been said, we only access a small percent of our brain; unless you happened to have some NZT-48. *NZT-48 is a fictional bootleg new drug that allows one hundred percent brainpower, or unlimited brain access from the movie "Limitless "*. The film's interesting premise is what could happen if we had one hundred percent brain capacity, being able to remember anything you have learned, heard, or seen, as well as to master any skill quickly. Another movie "Lucy" had a similar take.

What if we looked at time in the same way, what could happen if we had one hundred percent *time capacity*? What if we shifted out of that old paradigm (24 hours in a day), to the Patent **1440 Minute Countdown Clock,** where one hour becomes 60 minutes, or even 3,600 seconds! Two hours becomes 120 minutes or 7,200 seconds? Weekends become two thousand *waking minutes* long! Time has expanded exponentially by 6000%! Who doesn't have the time now? You become a witness of the amount of time you really have left in one day, one hour, or on the weekends. You become the observer of the matrix clock and therefore not controlled by it. You know it's Saturday, but that ancient Roman God "Saturn" is no longer in control of how you think or feel. You step out of linear time and alter your perception of clock-time itself. You alone become accountable for your time and measure it accordingly. You either want something more or you don't, always your choice of course.

1440TIME™ is your NZT-48 for time!

**"Things may come to those that wait, but only things left by those that hustle."**
—Abraham Lincoln

I know a lot of you work hard at your job, and when not there you're looking to do chores, relax, watch, or play sports. Go to the movies, see your kids play ball. Watch TV and have some fun, but unless you invest and spend *some* of your *"free"***On-Time** on your own personal growth, your life will have a somewhat predictable outcome. That's okay too if that's what you choose, but don't have an attitude at work, kick the cat, or blame Wall St.! It is what it is! Nevertheless, if you want more in this great game of life, **you must use some of your time, your mind, and the technology afforded to you.**

Start by cutting back on time spent on sports, movies, reality shows, soap operas, the radio, social networking sites, and Internet videos, and redirect just some of that time to more reading, writing, technology, and personal fitness and well-being. In other words, let's boost our share price and earnings, and watch our stock soar!

On the next few pages, we will begin to break down The 1440Power System®, showing you the three core zones of a day in the lives of millions of Americans and even the world.

1.  **Sleep**
2.  **Livelihood (work)**
3.  **On-Time (free time)**

**"Hard luck is composed of laziness, bad judgment, and poor execution."**
—joe-ks.com inspirational quotes

## MAX YOUR PERSONAL PRODUCTIVITY

## THE TRILOGY OF TIME

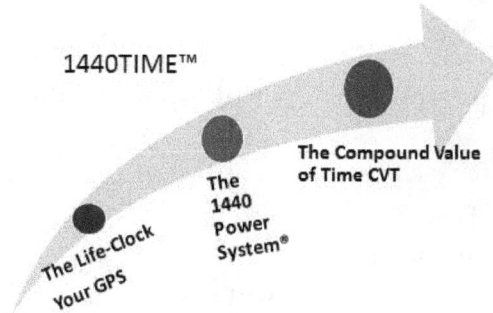

1440TIME™

The Compound Value of Time CVT

The 1440 Power System®

The Life-Clock Your GPS

1. **Life Clock** — (The Forest)
   - ° What time is it for you on the Great Clock of Life?
   - ° If not now, when?
2. **1440 Power System®**
   - ° The GTIME™ Voucher, good for 1,440 minutes each day only (EOT).
   - ° Your Minutes Create your Future
   - ° On-Time
   - ° PowerTime PT
   - ° PowerTime Plus PTP
   - ° 365togo Calendar
3. **Compound Value of Time**
   - ° The Power of Compounding Daily Minutes
   - ° 20 minutes a day = 3 full college courses in 1 year!
   - ° Daily Time Credit Deposits into your bank of knowledge and fitness.

## Breaking down the 1440 Power System®

**Sleep:**
- Rejuvenate the Mind and Body

**Livelihood**

- The price of the ticket into the game (A JOB)

**On-Time (OT):**

- Your Time!
- You Own this Time!
- You're not off of work, **you're On-Time**

When sleeping, sleep well, when working, work hard, so you can live a full and vigorous life, rich in experience.

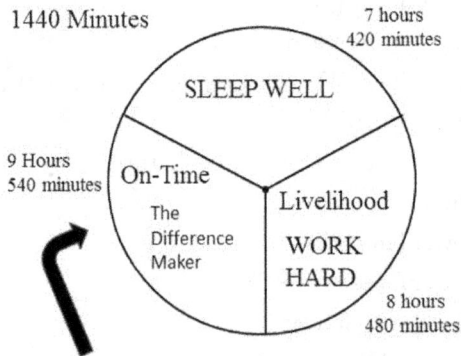

**"For every minute spent in organizing, an hour is earned."** —Harvey MacKay

## YES, A TEN-HOUR WORKDAY CAN BE LONG!

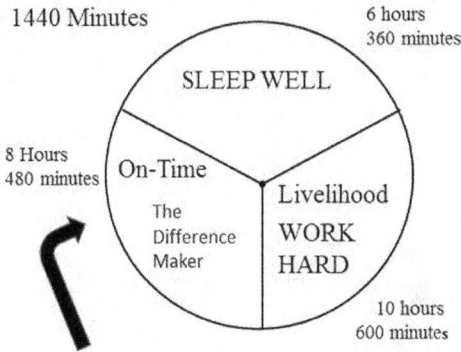

1440 Minutes

6 hours
360 minutes

SLEEP WELL

8 Hours
480 minutes   On-Time

The
Difference
Maker

Livelihood
WORK
HARD

10 hours
600 minutes

If this is your day, you still have 480 On-Time minutes to get the things done and more:

• 120 minutes family and home maintenance
• 60 minutes for educational purposes
• 40 minutes for working-out
• 120 minutes for television
• 140 minutes for miscellaneous

*This is not meant to be precise, it's to give you the frame work, a concept, and a guideline to what is possible in the world of 1440TIME™

**"It's how we spend our time here and now, that really matters. If you are fed up with the way you have come to interact with time, change it."**
— Marcia Wieder

# WORKING TWELVE HOURS TO LIVE SIX?

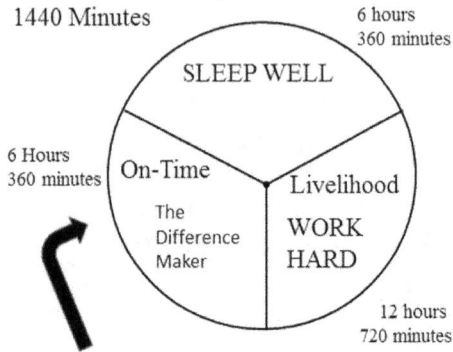

1440 Minutes

6 hours
360 minutes

SLEEP WELL

6 Hours
360 minutes

On-Time

The
Difference
Maker

Livelihood

WORK
HARD

12 hours
720 minutes

If this is your day, you still have 360 On-Time Minutes!

**Keys:**

1.  Utilize commute minutes to further your education by listening to audio books or using a tablet, if you use mass transit.
2.  Spend your 360 OT Minutes carefully. √
3.  Put additional free minutes in on your weekends. √
4.  Think about a new job or career. √
5.  Stay status quo.

**"Time is like money, the less we have of it to spare the further we make it go."**
—Josh Billings

# 17. TIME KEEPS ON SLIPPIN SLIPPIN' INTO THE FUTURE

Remember those lyrics from "Fly Like An Eagle" by the Steve Miller band? Of course, you do. The year was 1976, and Jimmy Carter defeated Gerald Ford for President.

Let us slip on into the future right now and look at a *weekend of time*. Each weekend—two complete days—is comprised of about two thousand waking minutes, give or take a few depending on the time you spend asleep. Multiply two thousand by fifty-two weeks per year, and you get over one hundred thousand minutes—the equivalent of the time you might spend during *six to eight years of a college* education and *we haven't the time to get in better shape, read more, or learn new skills?* Could it be that our Reticular Activating System is hard at work, and has assigned every weekend to be "off" days in our minds? Saturday (Saturn's Day) and Sunday (Sun's Day) are words that have developed meanings of their own. They are now synonymous with "non-work" days or "do what I want" days. Together they are supported by our thinking, based on automatic default programs of our subconscious minds. This is the routine clock that runs our lives fifty-two weekends a year, up until now that is…

**"There are never enough hours in a day, but always too many days before Saturday."**
—Hanson's Treatment of Time

The weekend is a time to get away from work (our livelihood); it's "our time" after all our hard work during the week, dealing with traffic, bosses, and the pressures of the job, we deserve this "free time" on these two days—don't we?

Perhaps not. Remember Pavlov's dog.

As you will see and learn, if you don't have 'much time' during your normal work week, it will be your weekends when "time optimization" will be paramount. Just 140 minutes a weekend, a little over an hour each Saturday and Sunday in one year adds up to the equivalent in time of three full college courses. In addition, since most of us don't work at our jobs on the weekends, we have an additional five hundred minutes of free time at our disposal!

Using The 1440 Power System® to have 'more' time on weekends feels good. But now multiply that by fifty-two weeks. That's a lot of minutes my friends! Weekend time is not **off-time**, it is **On-Time**, and is the time needed if you want to go for more in your life. And when you apply the Compounding Value of Time (CVT), you could be knowledgeable on almost any topic you choose in less than a year! You could also assign just sixty minutes every weekend for fitness and see the fruits of your labor transform your outlook on life! *Not so hard to do when you look at it this way, is it?*

**"The great dividing line between success and failure can be expressed in five words: "I did not have time."** —Franklin Field

# 18. THE 365togo CALENDAR

Now that you realize that **you do have the time**—usually over one thousand waking minutes daily—you can apply this time to the 365togo calendar for those longer-range goals of up to a year. The 365togo calendar expands on the breakdown system by reducing the burden of long, arduous goals.

Setting big goals wouldn't be such a bad thing if we didn't feel so overwhelmed by them. Many times we fly out of the gate when there's a goal we want, but after a few days or weeks our motivation wanes because the results don't seem to be coming quickly enough. What started out with the belief that we, too, could have that great body without working at it—or that the wealthy lifestyle we want is only three payments of $39.95 away, has faded due to the efforts, commitment, and the time required to meet that goal. That's why setting shorter and doable tasks using daily minutes compounded is the formula for completion of your targets. When you see 400 minutes left on your 1440 watch or app, you know you can find 20 or 30 to put in towards that goal. Again, it's called the "ownership clock" for a reason.

The 365togo calendar works by using an unconventional method based on our **calendar** system. The first step is to set the goal you want to reach. Be precise with your timelines, a start, and finish date! Then determine all the steps you'll need to complete this goal and write them down! Each day on the 365togo calendar is numbered as it would be on any calendar, but in this case, there's a twist. Each day shows the day of the month—1, 2, 3, and so on—then it indicates how many days are left in the year (starting at 365 and subtracting one each day).

### January 2014

| 1-365 Wednesday | 2-364 Thursday | 3-363 Friday | 4-362 Saturday |
|---|---|---|---|

So, each day has two numbers: the date and the number of days left in the year. What does this accomplish? It helps break the pattern of the traditional way we've always looked at the calendar, which is chronological by taking power away from the hypnotic trance of the word. Monday now becomes more than just the day we have to go back to work. It reminds you every day that you're either getting closer or further away from that *goal you set*. Every time you complete some part of your goal, no matter how small, make a strike through the numbers on your calendar.

Make time your workout partner and your assistant. Make time your best friend, and never under estimate **the power of compounding time!**

**"Time and I against any two."**
—Baltasar Gracian Quotes

| The Goal 365togo Calendar | | | | | | |
|---|---|---|---|---|---|---|
| JANUARY/FEBRUARY 2014 | | | | | | |

| | | | 1-365 WED | 2-364 THURS | 3-363 FRI | 4-362 SAT |
|---|---|---|---|---|---|---|
| 5-361 SUN | 6-360 MON | 7-359 TUES | 8-358 WED | 9-357 THURS | 10-356 FRI | 11-355 SAT |
| 12-354 SUN | 13-353 MON | 14-352 TUES | 15-351 WED | 16-350 THURS | 17-349 FRI | 18-348 SAT |
| 19-347 SUN | 20-346 MON | 21-345 TUES | 22-344 WED | 23-343 THURS | 24-342 FRI | 25-341 SAT |
| 26-340 SUN | 27-339 MON | 28-338 TUES | 29-337 WED | 30-336 THURS | 31-335 FRI | 1-334 SAT |
| 2-333 SUN | 3-332 MON | 4-331 TUES | 5-330 WED | 6-329 THURS | 7-328 FRI | 8-327 SAT |

The purpose of the 365togo calendar, like the book, is to keep you mindful of where you are now, and yet how much time (days) you have left in the year or goal you set forth for yourself. On the next page, you will see what a shorter-term goal might look like using the 365togo format using this example. Let's say you had a goal to get a certification using an online course starting February 1st and ending July 1st. The 365togo calendar would start at 150 and end at 0. You check off the declining number each day you accomplish some part of that goal you set for yourself.

**"The difference between a successful person and others is not a lack of strength, not a lack of knowledge, but rather a lack of will."**
—Vince Lombardi

## A goal would look like this.

| The Goal 365togo Calendar | | | | | | |
|---|---|---|---|---|---|---|
| Begin Goal FEBRUARY 2014 | | | | | | |
| | | | | | | 1-~~150~~<br>SAT |
| 2-~~149~~<br>SUN | 3-~~148~~<br>MON | 4-~~147~~<br>TUES | 5-~~146~~<br>WED | 6-~~145~~<br>THURS | 7-~~144~~<br>FRI | 8-~~143~~<br>SAT |
| 9-~~142~~<br>SUN | 10-~~141~~<br>MON | 11-~~140~~<br>TUES | 12-~~139~~<br>WED | 13-~~138~~<br>THURS | 14-~~137~~<br>FRI | 15-~~136~~<br>SAT |
| 16-~~135~~<br>SUN | 17-~~134~~<br>MON | 18-~~133~~<br>TUES | 19-~~132~~<br>WED | 20-~~131~~<br>THURS | 21-~~130~~<br>FRI | 22-~~129~~<br>SAT |
| 23-~~128~~<br>SUN | 24-~~127~~<br>MON | 25-~~126~~<br>TUES | 26-~~125~~<br>WED | 27-~~124~~<br>THURS | 28-~~123~~<br>SAT | 1-~~122~~<br>MARCH<br>20% |
| 2-~~121~~<br>SUN | 3-~~120~~<br>MON | 4-~~119~~<br>TUES | 5-~~118~~<br>WED | 6-~~117~~<br>THURS | 7-~~116~~<br>FRI | 8-~~115~~<br>SAT |

March (31-91)—April (30-61) —May (31-30)

| June 2014 | Completion of Goal July 1st 2014 | | | | July 2014 | |
|---|---|---|---|---|---|---|
| 1-~~29~~<br>SUN | 2-~~28~~<br>MON | 3-~~27~~<br>TUES | 4-26<br>WED | 5-25<br>THURS | 6-24<br>FRI | 7-~~23~~<br>SAT |
| 8-~~22~~<br>SUN | 9-~~21~~<br>MON | 10-20<br>TUES | 11-~~19~~<br>WED | 12-18<br>THURS | 13-~~17~~<br>FRI | 14-~~16~~<br>SAT |
| 15-~~15~~<br>SUN | 16-~~14~~<br>MON | 17-~~13~~<br>TUES | 18-~~12~~<br>WED | 19-~~11~~<br>THURS | 20-~~10~~<br>FRI | 21-~~9~~<br>LAST TEN<br>DAYS |
| 22-8<br>SUN | 23-7<br>MON | 24-6<br>TUES | 25-5<br>WED | 26-4<br>THURS | 27-~~3~~<br>FRI | 28-~~2~~<br>SAT |
| 29-~~1~~<br>SUN | 30-0<br>MON | July 1ST TUESDAY<br>*Goal Completed* | | | | |

## "Happiness is not a goal; it is a by-product."
—Eleanor Roosevelt

# 19. THERE IS NOTHING MORE DECEPTIVE THAN AN OBVIOUS CLUE

When Dr. Watson finally went to Sherlock Holmes after several days of trying to figure out a tough problem, Sherlock said, "There is nothing more deceptive than an obvious clue, Watson." He was right!

Sometimes the solutions to problems are so obvious we do not see them. Every day the brain takes in information, and we constantly make judgments, decisions, and assumptions based on that information. But are those assumptions correct? Or are there other alternatives? Do we see all there is to see?

We've all seen countless examples of this in mind games, perception illusions in books, and of course the hundreds of times we have forgotten where something is, only to realize it was right in plain sight, but is the greatest illusion of all, **time** itself?

Time should now be first in your mind. It's all part of the ultimate goal of activating your **T**ime **A**wareness **S**ystem™.

**"It is our illusions that create the world."**
—Didier Van Cauwelaert

In the movie *What The Bleep Do We Know!*, Dr. Joe Dispenza says, "Our brain takes in over four hundred billion bits of information per second but only processes about two hundred thousand bits per second." With this "bit" of information, we can easily see how obvious clues are easily overlooked—why we forget where we put our keys, only to remember that they're in our jacket pocket.

*Answer these questions:What color is a Stop sign? How many sides does it have?What color is a Yield sign? How many sides does it have?*

If you had to think a minute before answering, or if you just don't remember, you're not unusual. In fact, most people respond to these questions incorrectly, but it has nothing to do with their level of education or intelligence. It is just a simple example of our minds at work. We tend to take for granted the things we see every day—so much so that we stop thinking about their specific details and only assume they are as we remember them. It's a simple demonstration of the way our subconscious and conscious minds work. The subconscious mind acts much like a software program that produces documents; you set the page layout, margins, paragraphs, and fonts. When you save the document, the settings you chose become the default settings until you change them in the future. But if you never modify the configurations, they remain the same, just as a song remains the same no matter how often you play it. This is much like the program we still have in our minds when it comes to time and the twelve-hour standard clock and calendar system. The good news is that you also have a conscious mind, which is the critical factor. In fact, it's the mind you are using right now as you read this book, the one that governs your ability to think logically and to decide whether something makes sense to you or not.

And by the way, the Yield sign has been *red* for over forty years! Go to the link below and see for yourself?

http://the1440powersystem.blogspot.com/2017/06/are-we-living-world-of-yellow-yield.html

That's right, forty years! So why do so many of us see yellow yield signs in our minds when we pass red ones every single day?

In the same way, even though we see clocks and calendars every day, we see time through a filter that no longer serves our current condition. Just as we've been living in a world of three "f's" and yellow Yield signs for too long; we've been living in a world of old clocks and calendars for too long. Every time you see a Red Yield sign, and you will see many, this will trigger the question, am I present, in the now, in control, or am I living on someone else's time clock, some simulated reality from past civilizations' clocks and calendar systems?

**"People only see what they are prepared to see."** —Ralph W. Emerson

# 20. WE DON'T KNOW WHAT WE DON'T KNOW

In his book *The 8ᵗʰ Habit: From Effectiveness to Greatness*, Stephen Covey quotes maverick psychiatrist R. D. Laing: "The range of what we think and do is limited by what we fail to notice. And because we fail to notice that we fail to notice, there is little we can do to change; until we notice how failing to notice *shapes* our thoughts and deeds." Now read Laing's words again, oh how it fits for the way we fail to notice <u>time</u> in our lives today for <u>what it is</u>; therefore, there is little we can do to change, that is up until now. In the same book, Covey says, "Between stimulus and response, there is a space. In that space lies our freedom and power to choose our response. In those choices lie our growth and our happiness." Covey goes on to say that having an awareness of our freedom and power to choose is affirming because it can excite our "sense of possibility and potential." But that awareness can also seem threatening, even terrifying because suddenly it makes us feel responsible, or in Covey's words, "response-able." For the purposes of this book, let's add something to the last words of Covey's theorem. If awareness can seem threatening, even terrifying, because it suddenly makes us feel responsible, then our new perception of time could have the same effect. *But with that awareness also comes the responsibility that we can no longer use time as an excuse for why we didn't, couldn't, shouldn't, or can't do anything…ever again.*

To all my third-quarter friends, welcome! You are the ones who need this book *now*, and I'm right there with you! Look below, as I've added on to Bertrand Planes Life Clock.

## THE GAME CLOCK OF LIFE

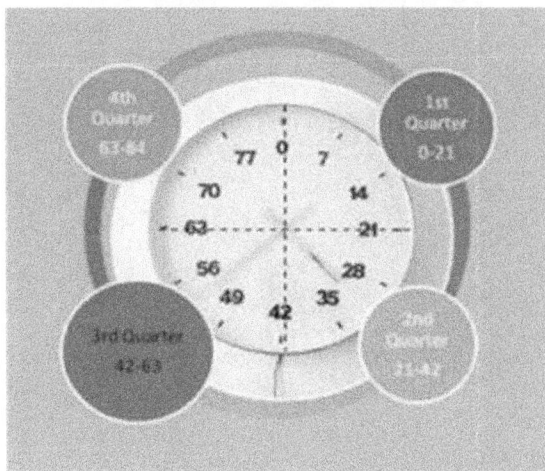

Since this is a motivational book, it's time for us to get moving. The time is now—not yesterday, last month, or twenty years ago. It's time to stretch yourself; exercise, learn more, read more, lose that weight, quit smoking, and drink less? Every 1440 minutes that goes by is one day gone on the great clock of life? If not now, when?

**"In the game of life, nothing is less important than the score at half time."**
—Anonymous

## The Game Clock of Life
## For All my Third-Quarter Players

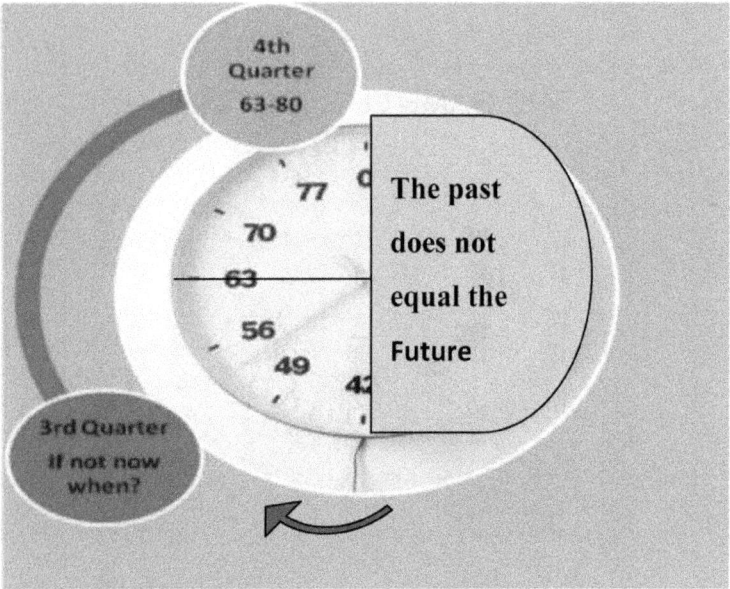

Look at the Game Clock of Life this way: The past is over, so all you have is to move forward. It's that simple. The 1440 Power System® will create your new today and your new future. On the other hand, where you are right now is where you will be in five, ten, or twenty years if you don't change your thoughts and actions today. Don't wait until the fourth quarter of the game clock to finally wake up, and if you're already in the fourth quarter, time is ticking! Let's get moving NOW!!

**"Defer no time, delays have dangerous ends."** —William Shakespeare

# 21. HOW ABOUT A NEW TIME GRID?

Maybe we need a new grid for the way we process time in America. We are already working on a new energy grid, admittedly at a snail's pace. But as President Obama said on his trip back Copenhagen in December 2009, "The time is now. We have been talking about change for the last two decades. It's time to stop talking—it's time to take action." It's eight years later 2017, how are we doing?

Our healthcare system needs a new grid, or at least a huge overhaul, as the Government fights over Obama care. Is it here to stay? In other parts of American life, the banks are back with plenty of cash; General Motors is back from the dead. And Google, Amazon, Facebook, and Apple cranking along. Twitter is trying to come back from its IPO price with the help of President Trump, news and sports media, while Snapchat is the new kid in town, trying to make it happen.

The need to increase and improve our use of alternative energy is paramount for the country's prosperity, and the need to revamp our healthcare system cannot be denied. In example after example, the old thinking of the past is not working anymore, and change is the answer. But for change to occur **we the people have to change first, for America to regain its foothold**—from driving more efficiently, to using technology better, to learning new skill sets, to changing the way we look at wellness, diet, and exercise. All of us will need to do more, and there is great power in numbers.

## ONE NATION OVERWEIGHT

I viewed a show on national television called *One Nation Overweight* a few years ago, but look around, who needs someone to tell us that we're an overweight nation and medical cost is skyrocketing?

- The annual healthcare cost of obesity in this country is $147 billion a year. This could rise to as much as $344 billion by 2018, according to one major study. Source CNBC One Nation Overweight
- 60% of Americans are classified as overweight or obese. Source Based on research by Kenneth E. Thorpe, Ph.D. of Emory University
- Obese employee sick days total approximately thirty-nine million workdays and sixty-three million doctor visits yearly. Source Vermont Department of Health

For now, in 2017 and 2018, how do we get tens of millions of Americans in better shape? How about giving money to get in shape? People do amazing things when cold hard cash is the incentive provided to get something done! Look at the TV show "The Biggest Loser" on NBC. Some of these people lose 200 pounds or more in the year, why? One reason is the amount money they can win!! If we can manage "cash for clunkers," why not "cash for healthy living"? I believe it can be done.

Say that you're forty pounds overweight; you go to the doctor on March 19, 2017 anytime before April 1, 2017 of the current year. The Doctor documents your weight at 225 lbs. At the end of the year (that is, in December 31, 2017), you go back, and the doctor confirms your new weight at 185 lbs. At that point, he signs the correct form from the IRS that says you are eligible for the healthy living tax credit ($3, 500) on your next year's tax return! You would bring that to your qualified tax preparer, CPA or Enrolled Agent when you file your return in the coming January. He or she checks the form and signs off on it as well. Wow!!! What a concept....

I know there would have to be parameters and rules set to qualify for this healthy living tax credit, but so what! There are rules for all the other tax credits as well, such as the first-time homebuyer credit, the earned income credit, and the college credits. Why couldn't we use this template as an incentive for people to quit smoking, lower hyper-tension, and blood pressure—basically anything that brings about a healthier mind and body? Of course, most people need motivation, some catalyst to get going. What better motivation than money?

It's evident that nothing else is working on a large scale. Imagine if just ten percent of the people in this country went on a health kick. Now imagine twenty or thirty percent! Sure, it may start out as a bid for more money, but think of the ongoing benefits and the long-range savings...trillions!!! From the bestselling book, *The 17-Day Diet* by Dr. Mike Moreno: "Get in shape and you can improve your financial shape too. It's considerably more expensive to be unfit than it is to be fit. Mainly because you're sicker more often and you pay higher medical bills." This is the type of forethought needed in this country right now, thinking outside the box and now we need to think outside the clock as well.

**"Large income is the best recipe for happiness I have ever heard."** —Jane Austin

This book is not about how to lose weight or create jobs; it is not about how to get rich or be smart. It's not telling you to stop watching sports or your favorite TV shows or to stop visiting Facebook. This book deals with the now and makes you aware that you have plenty of time for all that stuff, with enough left over to go for more and increase your own personal successes. Maybe even to leave that job you don't like one day, or have that house, car or vacation you have always wanted!

The Time Factor doesn't tell you how to do something, or get something, but will give you the *time* to do and get anything you desire.

- It doesn't tell you how to make more money, but gives you the time to learn how to make more money.
- It doesn't tell you how to prepare for the future, but it will give you the time to learn how to prepare for the future
- It doesn't teach you how to learn about finances, but it gives you the time to learn about finances.
- It doesn't tell you how to get physically fit, but it will give you the time to learn about fitness and the time to become more fit.

**"Our progress as a nation can be no swifter than our progress in education."**
—John F. Kennedy

# 22. IF IT'S WORTH LIVING IT'S WORTH WRITING DOWN

**"The discipline of writing something down is the first step toward making it happen."**
—Lee Iacocca

What if the ancient Egyptians had acted like most of us today? There would have be very little historical data from those times available today. What would the history books look like? The Cro-Magnon never left written records, so we don't know much about them. Historical events had no real value to the Cavemen, so it made little sense to write about them. Besides, it would have taken too much time and effort. Are we much different from the Cavemen? How many people write diaries, journals, or anything at all? How many record their goals, dreams and life? Why bother? It doesn't make much sense, unless the writing is your livelihood. Who wants to write without being paid, or at least the chance of being paid?

Back in the late'80s, I was at one of Anthony Robbins' seminars when he said, "If it's worth living, it's worth writing down." It took me a long time to fully understand, appreciate, and apply Tony's words, but I realize now that back then I was too close to the trees to see the forest.

Consistently writing down your thoughts validates them; the way a stamp does for a letter. No stamp…No delivery…Storing your thoughts in some form is the only way to preserve their power and energy for future use, in the same way that pictures capture memories of times past and preserves them for the future to enjoy; also people who write down their goals usually have more successes. However, do not delay—immediate action is required. When those inspired moments arise, or something you need to do pops into your head, go write it down! All the great ideas in the world mean nothing, if we don't save them. Yes, those dreams, thoughts, ideas, and goals wind up in the *lost-and-found department of the universe of unsaved intellectual property.*

You know how frustrating it is when you're in the process of doing some work on your computer and a system error occurs. Yikes! All of a sudden you realize that you haven't saved the document and now it's *gone.* This happened to me during a tax season a few years ago when I was working on a long Schedule D form, which lists the sale of stocks. I'd already inputted over 350 trades, a task that had taken me the better part of four hours (240 minutes) when the error message appeared. Yup, you guessed it. I'd forgotten to save my work, because I'd been so engrossed in the process. Believe me, I learned my lesson. Now I save things quickly and often, especially when they're compelling thoughts or when that flash of genius hits my brain.

**"Write down the thoughts of the moment. Those that come unsought for are commonly the most valuable."** —Francis Bacon, Sr.

## INFORMATION OVERLOAD

Trying to keep ideas in our heads for any length of time can seem futile, given the complexity of life today when information overload and *Time Inflation* are at an all-time high.

What's "Time Inflation"? Time Inflation occurs when we spend more and more time doing things that don't serve us. Examples would include too much TV, sports, Facebook, YouTube, coffee clutching, bars and even running the kids all over the place. In the end, the cost of our time inflates, leaving less and less time for things that really count, like goals, dreams, and our future.

*When You Control the Clock—You Control the Game*

In a *Success Magazine* interview, Steven Covey says, "Writing things down is a psycho neuro muscular activity that **imprints the subconscious mind.**" I can use the example of riding a bicycle, a physical muscular activity that imprints the physical body. But whether it's a goal, a dream, or just physical fitness you desire, some form of muscular activity is required.

*I've got it, Holmes!* If the missing common denominator is a muscular activity, either physical or psycho-neural in nature, then it's obvious that if we want to become more physically fit we must exert a physical muscular activity, and if we want to attain our goals and reach our dreams, we must exert a psycho-neuromuscular activity, perhaps by writing down our goals and dreams in physical form.

*Splendid, my dear Watson, as there is nothing more deceptive than an obvious clue!*

## THINK LIKE A GOLFER

Thinking like a golfer means keeping a scorecard. If you track the progression of your game throughout the year, you'll either find yourself getting closer to your goals…or you won't. Let's review the changes we must to make:

- Change the hours we have in a day to minutes we have left in a day and know where you are using 1440TIME™;
- Subtract the time we spend asleep to get the number of waking minutes we have left on the 1440Clock™, *known as your base waking time rate;*
- Put down our thoughts and goals in material form on a consistent basis to activate the psycho-neuromuscular activity that imprints our subconscious mind. This is where the birth of thought begins its journey;
- Avoid mental laziness. How long does it take to jot down a thought, a goal or a dream every once in a while? A few minutes of your time;
- Avoid physical laziness. Get up and go, it's G-Time™ even if it's just running around the block once a day. We're not all training to be Olympic athletes.
- Realize and recognize The 1440 Power System® has three zones; **Sleep—Livelihood—ON-TIME.**
- Understand the power of the **"Compound Value of Time (CVT)** *"Your minutes compounded daily, create your future"*

**"Nothing is more terrible than activity without insight."** —Thomas Carlyle

# 23. SO WHAT YOU DO FOR A LIVING?

Someone recently asked me what I do for a living. Instead of responding in the way 99.9 percent of the population would—with a job description—I said, "I sleep for 360 minutes, get up at 6:00 am, have a cup of coffee, turn on the computer, write or read until about 7:00, then go down to the basement to workout. By 8:00, I've made breakfast for my family (most days) and have taken a shower." When I stopped to catch my breath, the questioner interjected, "*Stop*! That's not what I meant. What do you do to pay your bills? You know *your job*!" "Oh," I said, "I have a tax preparation company, and I help people with investing ideas."

Do *you* define your life by what you do for a living? I am an electrician. I am a network specialist. I am a painter. I work at Home Depot. I am a secretary. I am a doctor. These are all job descriptions, sure, but really, they are nothing more than default answers that define what we do as a means of support, livelihood! Your livelihood zone is for working and paying for the ticket into the great park of life.

**"Work harder on yourself than you do on your job."** —Jim Rohn

Is this subconscious default program defining our lives by the job we have? Do you remember Pavlov's dog?

**"A job is really a short-term solution for a long term problem."**
—Robert Kiyosaki from Rich Dad Poor Dad

Recently I watched a "protocol expert" on television. This authority on etiquette described the correct way to greet someone:

"Start with the handshake and some small talk. 'Hi, my name's Kevin. What's your name?' 'Bill.' 'Nice to meet you, Bill. What do you do for a living?'"

Even the experts have decided that this is what we're supposed to say. If you're in a sales position, working your business, by all means stay with the status; "what do you do for a living"?

The word "living" (as defined by Merriam-Webster) is "a condition of being alive; full of life and vigor; having a life; to have a life rich in experience." The dictionary does not say, "Living: real estate agent, police officer, or left tackle for the New York Giants." So, the next time someone asks you, "What do you do for a living?" you might say, "Oh, you mean what is my job?"

For most of us, work amounts to about one-third of our day of our entire 1440 minutes we get. We work to buy food, clothing, and put a roof over our heads, and for the amenities, safety, and privilege of living in these great United States. Do we appreciate this third of day enough, or are we on some automatic pilot going through the motions of work life, **doing time** until we can retire sometime in the future?

Those who do what they love and figure out a way to make it their livelihood, have combined **On-Time** with **Work Time** in a powerful way. People in this position often make more money, are happier and live a life richer in experiences.

For many others, however, their work (livelihood) is just a job, and when they're not at work they're in the *Free-Time* zone, those precious minutes when they're not working or sleeping. But "free-time" is an oxymoron! You may be free from work-time, but there is no free-time allotted on the Game Clock of Life. Once gone, it's gone forever.

We get one ticket, one life, and a big 1440 minutes daily to use wisely!

**"Time is free, but it's priceless. You can't own it, but you can use it. You can't keep it, but you can spend it. Once you've lost it you can never get it back."** —Harvey McKay

The old hourly wage—the nine-to-five, Monday-through-Friday schedule with weekends off—is no more than an adjunct to our *outdated time grid*. And even though many companies like Apple and Google constantly reinvent their work environments to promote vision and creativity among their employees, the vast majority of workers are paid by the hour, and their employers provide few incentives to go for more.

I just got done working for a painting company for over five months, while doing research for this book, and there were certainly no incentives provided, outside of the fact you got paid every Friday. Is the daily grind and robot thinking, what it's all about?

We should be paid for the value we bring to sixty minutes, or output per hour, not just for punching an employee time clock!

Check out the book **5-Hour Work day by Stephan Aarstol**. He was on the Shark Tank and his company uses a new model for employee working hours 8:00 AM - 1:00 PM. Stephan is spot on, so get his book and learn more about his take on working in the new age world, where people are looking for more than just a JOB!

**"If you are not willing to risk the unusual, you will have to settle for the ordinary."** —Jim Rohn

## KILLING TIME

I know a plumber at a university who has mastered the art of killing time over and over again. He knows what work has to be accomplished every day and exactly how long it will take. And since he gets paid by the hour, he has little reason to make any more effort than is expected of him.

I also had clients who received unemployment insurance income for over a year. When I asked them what they had done with all that free time, most said, "nothing"!

"Nothing?" I said "You had over 350,000 free minutes, and you have nothing to show for it!"

When are we going to break out of our everyday habits? Perhaps the new economic optimism in America now, will be just the jolt we need to get people hungry again for that entrepreneurial spirt we once had.

**"When you play, play hard; when you work, don't play at all."** —Theodore Roosevelt

For those people who take their jobs seriously and use their work time to produce maximum results, there is no such thing as "killing time." If you are self-employed, I guarantee that you don't have time to kill. You probably learned early on that you had to make time your ally, use it properly or lose money, and maybe even your livelihood. Perhaps without knowing it, you've already been utilizing the 1440 Power System®! This book for you time masters is just icing on the cake. However, if you work by the hour in a job with no incentive to go for more, you're still burning through the same 1440 minutes you have every day. Regardless of your pay grade or the kind of job you have, you can still make effective use of your time while in this zone (livelihood). This is what the 1440 Power System® does. A day is just 1440 minutes whether you're working, sleeping or On-time! If you are not happy with your livelihood zone then work on changing it in your On-Time zone!!

Work as hard as you can. Raise the level of your game, get noticed, and good things are bound to happen.

---

**TIME VOUCHER**
**Redeem today only!!!**
Good for 1440 minutes

**Not valid tomorrow**

---

"**Men talk of killing time, while time quietly kills them.**" —Dion Boucicault

## TIME FACTORS

Your days, each comprised of 1,440 minutes are divided into three zones to accommodate sleep, work, and time spent on other pursuits. If you are *serious* about going for more in your life **On-Time** is where it starts.

As humans, we all have to sleep, we all have to work (in one capacity or another), and we all have that third zone of "free time." The latter is called your daily **On-Time**.

This next chapter expands our view of the 1440 Power System® inside the playing field of the Game of Life (the content), taking an even broader view of what a day really looks like. This is where PowerTime and PowerTime Plus are found, and are the key for ridding yourself of what I call the Time's Fault Syndrome (TFS) and other time-related stress disorders.

**"Time is the scarcest resource of the manager; If it is not managed, nothing else can be managed."** —Peter F. Drucker

By the time you're done with this book, you will realize that your job is just part of the 1440 Power System®. It pays for the ticket into the game; the other two-thirds of your day are for sleep (*repairing the cells and resting the mind and body*), and **On-Time**, (the difference maker) is for DOING AND GOING FOR MORE! **It's G-Time™!**

Take a look below, **The 1440 Power System®** at-a-glance, also the playing field of life (the content).

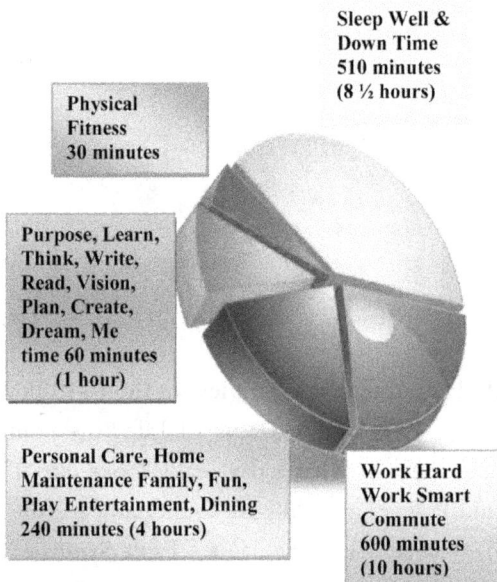

**Sleep Well & Down Time 510 minutes (8 ½ hours)**

**Physical Fitness 30 minutes**

**Purpose, Learn, Think, Write, Read, Vision, Plan, Create, Dream, Me time 60 minutes (1 hour)**

**Personal Care, Home Maintenance Family, Fun, Play Entertainment, Dining 240 minutes (4 hours)**

**Work Hard Work Smart Commute 600 minutes (10 hours)**

**"For disappearing acts, it's hard to beat what happens to the eight hours supposedly left after eight of sleep and eight hours of work."**
—Doug Larson

## NOTE:

All grids, charts, work schedules, Smart Clocks, and the Life Clock presented so far are there to assist you in the activation of your Time Awareness System™ (TAS). They're not intended to be factual representations of everyone's life. I know that many live in different cities and suburbs—some have longer commutes and travel more, while others work at home or around the block. People are single, divorced, or married with children; many are single parents. That said, time never changes; everyone has the same 1,440 minutes a day. **The only difference is how your minutes are divided between Sleep, Work, and On-Time.** It is up to you to apply time clock management. I just want you to be able to enjoy your lifetime ticket to the fullest, and the only way to do that is one day at a time, 1,440 minutes a day.

1440TIME™

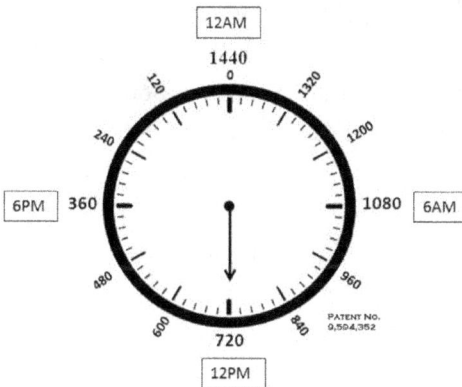

# 24. THE TIME VALUE OF TIME

**"A man who dares to waste one hour of life has not discovered the value of life."**
—Charles Darwin

What is the true Time Value of Time? This can be a difficult question until we see time for what it is and understand its true nature. Some of us have jobs that pay by the time (like attorneys who are paid by the minutes (where minutes x knowledge = their fee), while others are paid an hourly wage, regardless of the amount of work they produce each hour. But there are only two possibilities open to you if you are thinking about making more money. **"Either you invest some of your ON-TIME Minutes in a part-time job, or into things that could bring you more money down the road, such as higher education...or you do not."** It isn't wrong if you choose to spend your On-Time minutes (300 to 600 of them daily) in other pursuits like watching TV, going to the gym, doing chores, taking the kids places, going out to the local hangout, or just to relax—but they don't make you any money either. If you really want to make more money now or in the future, you must use some of your *On-Time Minutes* available to do it in. That is, unless you're getting royalty, dividend or rent checks while you're asleep.

Here's the bottom line. When you're awake you're either making money or you're not! *"I don't know what you're saying Kevin, what do you mean? The time I spend playing with my kids, cutting the grass, having fun with friends, watching a football game—these are all important too. Time isn't just about money, you know!"* You're right! It's about all those things you're doing, and more. But the fact remains: **you're either making money or you're not with your time!**

If you choose *not* to use any of your On-Time minutes to make more money now or to invest in future possibilities, your financial future is quite predictable. And complaining about it will only get you more of the same.

Time is money and money is time, but you have to decide which is worth more. It's your lifetime ticket and you only get one! You can spend it any way you choose, just remember there are no rollover minutes given to anyone.

The great news is now that your TAS is activated, and you understand the Compound Value of Time (CVT), you don't have to give up everything and change your whole life around, all you have to do is apply *ten to twenty percent of your On-Time minutes daily to a goal*, and the results will take care of themselves.

**"Between work and family, I'm really not spending enough quality time with my money."**
—Unknown

## The Three Zones of the 1440 Power System®

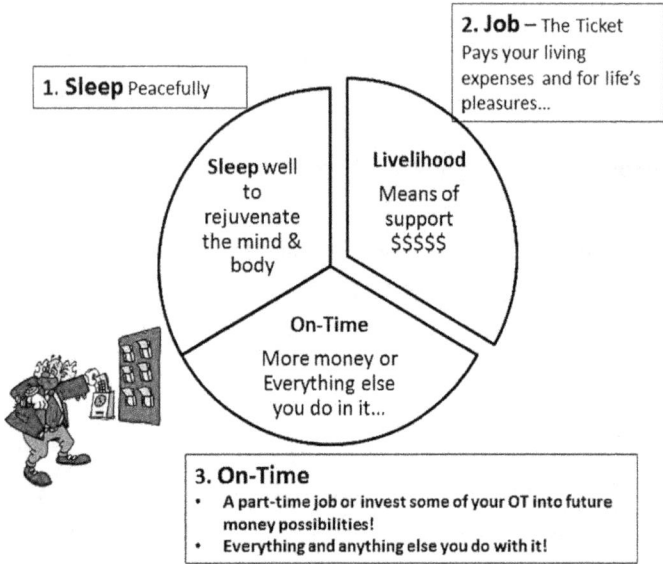

**1. Sleep** Peacefully

**2. Job** – The Ticket Pays your living expenses and for life's pleasures...

**Sleep** well to rejuvenate the mind & body

**Livelihood** Means of support $$$$$

**On-Time** More money or Everything else you do in it...

**3. On-Time**
- A part-time job or invest some of your OT into future money possibilities!
- Everything and anything else you do with it!

On-Time (formerly known as free-time) is where time becomes a valuable tool and asset. It is the time to go for more, *I call it GTIME™*, or we don't. The choice is yours. All I offer is the truth nothing more...The Blue pill or the Red pill...

**"The poor and the middle-class work for money. The rich have money work for them."**
—Robert Kiyosaki

If you have a job that gives you an annual cost-of-living raise, a simple "time value of money" calculation will tell you how much you will be making some time in the future. If you want to make more money beyond your current salary and annual raise, you will have to use some of your On-Time minutes to do it, either by getting a second job or by investing some of your On-Time minutes in things that could make you more money down the road. This could even mean educating yourself on financial matters, gaining knowledge about how money works—which would be a plus for your balance sheet. Let's say you have a part-time job for ten hours a week—that's an incredible 600 minutes. When you multiply those 600 minutes by fifty-two weeks you get 31, 200 minutes a year. Multiply that by two years and you get a whopping 62, 400 minutes—the time equivalent of more than four years of college! What do you have to show for your part-time, ten-hours-a-week job; after taxes, gas and lost time away from family, friends, education, and physical fitness? I'd venture to say little or nothing. I'd also say that your financial picture barely budged. But what if, you took those ten hours a week (31, 200 minutes), and applied them to health, fitness, and financial education! How much better off you would be today?

The Time Value of Time puts a different spin on the concept that time is money. In a very real sense, it is! So, don't under-appreciate, underestimate, undervalue, or undermine the great hidden power of time.

**"The key is in not spending time, but in investing it."** —Stephen R. Covey

In my tax business, if a simple return takes me fifteen minutes and costs $100 and I do four returns in an hour, I make $400 an hour. But if a client starts chatting with me, and I listen for ten minutes and respond for five minutes, I'll have lost $100 in the blink of an eye. If this goes on for thirty minutes, I'll have lost $200; after forty-five minutes, $300. The client still intends to pay the $100 for the "simple return" service whether it's one hour or 30 minutes, *so have I lost money, or did I lose time?*

Bear in mind that each tax season is only about one hundred and ten thousand declining minutes long (11 weeks)! And thinking in terms of minutes declining, helps me keep in mind that time is not only money, but my livelihood as well. Using the 1440TIME™ declining time clock model during my tax season has me at the very top of my game being one of H&R BLOCK's most productive Tax Pro's in the company. It is virtually impossible for someone who calibrates by hours and works on Saturday & Sunday to be me! I can work 16 hours on a Saturday or a Sunday with no problem. Those words have no power over me, they are just another 1440 minutes in another day.

Let's get you up to speed on the Time Value of Money concept— how time and money correlate in finances and in life. Start with this simple Time Value of Money example: *If you start with a thousand dollars and add an additional hundred dollars a month over ten years at 12 percent interest, the future value of your investment is $26,304.*

So what started out as an initial investment of $1,000, *(small amount)* and then by adding $100 monthly(even smaller) over ten years(time), has **grown** and **compounded** to **$26,304**.

Einstein dubbed it the Eighth Wonder of the World and said, "The most powerful force in the universe is compound interest."

# 25. CONCENTRATE ON YOUR GAME NOT THE GAME OF OTHERS

You're on a plane, getting ready to take off. The flight attendant, as usual, reads from her script. "If the plane loses pressure for any reason, the oxygen mask will drop down from the small overhead compartment. If that happens, pull the line and put the mask over your nose and mouth, relax, and breathe normally. If you have a child or someone who needs your help, put your own mask on first."

The same principle applies in life; many of us spend excessive amounts of time thinking about what others are doing, instead of focusing on what we should be doing. If your sports team loses so be it, get over it... Why get stressed out! You wind up losing valuable meaningful time because you're angry and you're not even getting paid or better yet, you're losing money because you can't concentrate on work! Concentrate on *your* game first; then you will be in a better position to help others.

Remember, as 1440TIME™ & The 1440 Power System® start to take over your thinking process, you will have more time for yourself and others than you ever thought possible.

**"Busy souls have no time to be busybodies".** —Austin O'Malley

## LESS IS MORE

It's time to clean out the basement, get rid of the clutter, and free up some mind space. You've heard it said that "less is more" and that there's "addition by subtraction," right? I apply these axioms to my life every day, focusing on *doing more in fewer defined areas*, the areas that count most in this great Game of Life. This is where **PowerTime Plus** (PTP) comes in to play—defined minutes x focused action = **Exponential results**. When in PTP amazing results happen, and you need less time to do it in.

Like many of you, I am in my third quarter now, and time has become increasingly more valuable. Would you not agree?

Do things that help you become more productive, intelligent, and physically sound. Cut out or at least cut down on the things and the people who detract or distract you from your vision, goals, and personal growth. Don't let things, the media, or others take up parking space in your head.

Remember, this book is the ultimate time management book and cures Times Fault Syndrome (TFS). It gives you the time to read great works by Tony Robbins, Jack Canfield, Eckhart Tolle, Dr. Stephen Covey, Napoleon Hill, Stephan Aarstol, and Jillian Michaels (Unlimited) to name just a few. It gives you the time to get to the gym, or work out at home. It gives you time to go for more!!!

**"Never confuse motion with action."**
—Benjamin Franklin

# FOCUS ON YOUR GAME...THE BEST GAME IN TOWN.

So many people waste time and energy on things that are meaningless, or over which they have little or no control. They sabotage their own game and wonder why things are not clicking. Think about this:

What does your sports team winning or losing have to do with your physical fitness?

What does Hollywood have to do with you reading more books?

What do the financial scandals have to do with you learning about investing?

What does Facebook have to do with you using the Internet as a powerful tool for self-education?

Are we doing what we should be doing every day to live a prosperous and healthy life? The stock markets and the economy are not the reasons why we can't prosper and thrive. When you are in the act of creating, there is nothing that can get in your way.

"Each player must accept the cards life deals him or her: but once they are in hand, he or she alone must decide how to play the cards in order to win the game." —Voltaire quotes

## LIFE AS CHESS

Try thinking about your Life-Time like a game of chess, and play your current moves by using your *time-vouchers* precisely and thoughtfully. Always anticipate the next move—then the one after that...and the one after that.

In this great Game of Life, each of us has the same 1,440 minutes a day to do, become, or create whatever we desire. If you don't have any desires, then the old clock will suit you just fine.

What is your purpose? Why do you think you are here? I know it's not easy to think about when life can get in the way. I mean who doesn't have challenges? Who doesn't have a TV? Who isn't getting information sent to them from all types of sources? You remember Effort Control from earlier? Google it and learn more about it!

We live in exciting, interesting, and thought-provoking times. There will be difficulties, but when we step back and see what we really have, it's clear we are living in amazing times. The game of sitting back, coasting, and depending on others to manage our retirement, our health, our career, and our life is old news. It won't work anymore. Take charge of your life and let the internet and technology work for you. That means get smarter!! Sure, you can still use it for pleasure and convenience, but save some time for advancing your intellect.

**"In the book of life, the answers aren't in the back."** —Charlie Brown

# 26. THE LAST MINUTE OF THE GAME

**"The tragedy of life is not that it ends so soon, but that we wait so long to begin it"**
—Anonymous

A sense of urgency is a great motivating tactic, especially in sports; the last minute of a football game, the last ten seconds of a basketball game, or the overtime in a hockey game. Each player goes all out because it's do-or-die time. What is it about some of these athletes that cause them to perform feats of greatness when they're under extreme pressure and the clock is running out—as the fans hang in the balance, anticipating the outcome? Just imagine if we could live our lives with **one-tenth** of the intensity these athletes do when they're playing those last ticks of the game clock! How much more could we do or become? What if we used just one-tenth more of our weekly time to go for more (GTIME it)? That equates to only about 100 minutes, since there are 10,800 minutes per week. So, who doesn't have the time to read, write, exercise, or learn more?

Did time slow down for Wayne Gretzky and Michael Jordan? Was the game speed just a bit slower for them than the other players? Is it possible that we can learn to slow the game of life down in our minds the way the greatest athletes do, by shifting to 1440TIME™!? Freeing ourselves from the outdated clock and hour system handed to us from centuries gone by?

Our current realities are filled with the benefits of instant gratification from smartphones to microwaves, but because we expect everything now, we have lost our patience along the way. Having it right now has become the new normal, anything less is not acceptable. We blame others and get angry when someone cuts us off while driving, the package we are waiting for is a day late, and the tax refund is delayed by three days. **We are living in a high-speed tech world, while our minds are still calibrated to an ancient world clock system,** not being able to make the connection that, "modern times, need a modern TIME system".

In this great game of life, we each have only so many minutes in the game. *Make this your two-minute warning*. Pick up the urgency, employ time management, take a chance, and start to think outside the box, and **Think Outside the Clock**™, that is no more hours, just minutes you have left in your day!

There are no more excuses and certainly time cannot be used as one. No one really has any advantage over you. We all have the tech tools and the brains at our disposal right now to achieve success.

*Time is the greatest tool and asset of all time*

Go to www.1440time.com to see more. Learn how to use tools and techniques that will show you how to get in-the-zone with time, by slowing the game clock down.

**"Don't let what you cannot do interfere with what you can do."** —John Wooden

# 27. THE PASSION OF TIME

Anthony Robbins personifies passion. For decades this motivational master has helped people around the world ignite their passion and live their dreams. I have had the privilege of attending many of Tony's seminars and workshops, have read all his books, and listened to his monthly PowerTalk cassettes back in the early '90s—a big favorite of mine. I could not wait for a new cassette and book summary to arrive each month. In these works, Tony interviews inspirational leaders, cutting-edge thinkers, and people who went from the depths of failure and despair to extraordinarily successful lives. I still remember the interview Tony had with Duane Chapman, known as the 'Dog' the Bounty Hunter. I had never heard of the 'Dog' back then, but I do know who he is now.

**Passion** is a driving force; it has always been that way. Without passion, we live a humdrum life. Why can't we live life with passion every day? Sure, it's easy to be inspired short term by movies with triumphant endings, songs with cool lyrics, and sounds or victories by your sports team. But what happens when the thrill wears off? In no time, the passion wanes and you're back to thinking inside the box, to the tune of "same old, same old."

*"Passion is the genesis of genius."* —Anthony Robbins

I have created this book to share this knowledge with you, so you can start to utilize time as the driving force to ignite your lasting passion from within. Many people have great ideas about how to improve something, make it easier or safer. Or a great idea for a story but fail to write it down and take action.

The Internet has become a distribution channel. Use your gold-mind to create a gold mine (e.g. Google+, Facebook and Twitter), bringing your thoughts to light for the world to see. You do not have to reinvent the wheel. Consider these few flashes of genius that have made it big: Facebook, Twitter, Angies List, GoPro, fuhu, Anchor Free, Coin, Foursquare, Headblade, 99¢ Only Stores, The Life is Good® Company, Mommy Millionaire, Silly Bandz, TOMS®, and Snapchat.

Successful people have learned to **fail forward fast**. When something isn't working, they aren't afraid to change course and move on swiftly. With 1440TIME™, you now have more time to think, write down your ideas, and cultivate a winning strategy for success, and if your plan doesn't work or needs tweaking, you will have the time now to make the changes and move on quickly.

Go read Jack Canfield's **The Success Principles** How to Get from Where You Are to Where You Want to Be. It has new updated material for our changing times and offers a comprehensive guide to "Success in the Digital Age".

You are now more than ready for this great game of life, knowing the rules and playing to win. You remember the formula: daily minutes x focused action = Exponential Results. Just twenty minutes a day equals seventy-three hundred minutes in one year, which is more than three and a half thirteen-week college courses. When combined with the main ingredient, "passion", you will be unstoppable—having results instead of reasons of why not...

**"We didn't lose the game; we just ran out of time."** —Vince Lombardi

# 28. THE VISION OF THE TIME

**"Nothing contributes so much to tranquilizing the mind as a steady purpose—a point on which the soul may fix its intellectual eye."**
—Mary Wollstonecraft Shelley

Vision means seeing something in your mind's eye first and setting your sights on the outcome in advance. In other words, mapping your own destiny!

When I was five years old, I got my first real understanding of vision while visiting my grandparents in Florida. The year was 1966, and Gramps was excited to show my two brothers and me a new park that was going to be built. We drove for about an hour, and all the way there Gramps told us about this magnificent park called Disney World. He described how huge it would be, the size of the landscape, the massive rides, the hotels. He talked about the theme characters in costumes everywhere you looked, roaming the park with balloons. He said that the biggest firework display we'd ever see would end each night. We were excited, but when we got there all we saw were acres and acres of land. Nothing else. Just land for as far as we could see. "Gramps," I said, "There's nothing here!" "Just close your eyes, son," said Gramps, "and imagine. Over there, that's the Magic Kingdom... and there, that's Cinderella's Castle...and over there, that's Epcot, where you'll fly in space and see the moon. And right over there—why that's Mickey and Minnie Mouse with all their friends!"

"I see it, Gramps," I exclaimed, "What an amazing and wonderful place this Disney World is. Who built it?" "Walt Disney," said Gramps. "A man with a great imagination and great vision."

Gramps had given us a first-hand demonstration of how to use our imagination and vision, and we never forgot the lesson.

Walt Disney saw the park in his mind long before it was built. All the obstacles, lack of financing, and critics could not derail his vision. He had clarity and focus, and it was just a *matter of time* before the greatest park of all would open for the world to see.

When the mind is in a place where imagination and vision rule, time shifts—a sense of timelessness takes over. Time seems not to exist, like "a purpose or point on which the soul may fix its intellectual eye."

We all have some purpose, something that we can fix our intellectual eye on, whatever it may be for each of us. So, what's your vision? One thing is for certain, *Equal Opportunity Time*, "EOT". We all have the same amount of time in a day, most have access to the internet, but without a vision, we are but mere spectators watching others do it.

**"It is a terrible thing to see and have no vision."**
—Helen Keller

## IN THE TIME-ZONE

Time spent in the zone utilizes both the Time value of Time (how much you love doing what you're doing) and the Compound Value of Time: Daily Minutes x Focused Action = Exponential Results (dm x fa= ER)

- Exponential growth vs. linear growth
- Fiber optics vs. dial-up connection.

**Exponential Growth—Time Value of Time**

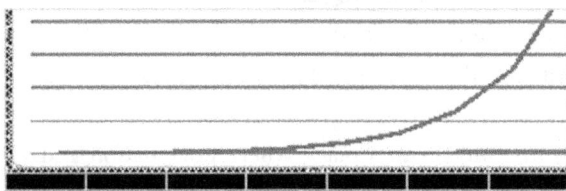

Linear Growth = **the 12-hour standard clock of today**

The old standard clock system still used today is linear, (chronological), while 1440TIME™ & The 1440 Power System® are the new paradigms needed for explosive personal productivity growth for the 21st century. This natural progression is imminent and the time is right now.

 **"The sign on the door of opportunity reads PUSH."** —Unknown

## KEEP SCORE

When golfers don't keep a scorecard to track their handicap, it usually means they are not too serious about their game. The ones that do take golf seriously always keep score. Doing so validates their handicap for club tournaments or pickup games; it helps them track their progress so they can see whether their game is improving or not. Why can't we think about "our time" the way we might think about our golf game?

If you believe your time is important and you're serious about it, keep a scorecard and track your progress to see whether your game is improving or not. Start by keeping score of your daily On-Time minutes (300-500 weekly and 2000+ on the weekends); assign fifteen, twenty, thirty or sixty of them to your goal or something new and different daily or weekly. Remember now that your TAS has been activated it cannot be reversed. You either see time as an opportunity, (*time to go for more*) or you will see time as a limitation (*conformity-status quo*). The choice is yours, not mine or anyones.

### The Ultimate Scorecard

| DATE: | HOLE | 1 | 2 | 3 | 4 | 5 | 6 | 7 | 8 | 9 | FRONT | 10 | 11 | 12 | 13 | 14 | 15 | 16 | 17 | 18 | BACK | TOTAL | ⚐ |
|---|---|---|---|---|---|---|---|---|---|---|---|---|---|---|---|---|---|---|---|---|---|---|---|
| | LENGTH | | | | | | | | | | | | | | | | | | | | | | |
| PLAYERS | PAR | | | | | | | | | | | | | | | | | | | | | | +/- |
| 1 | | | | | | | | | | | | | | | | | | | | | | | |
| 2 | | | | | | | | | | | | | | | | | | | | | | | |
| 3 | | | | | | | | | | | | | | | | | | | | | | | |
| 4 | | | | | | | | | | | | | | | | | | | | | | | |
| 5 | | | | | | | | | | | | | | | | | | | | | | | |
| 6 | | | | | | | | | | | | | | | | | | | | | | | |

**You are either winning or losing!**

## PLAY THE BALL

In baseball, if the shortstop waits for the ball to play him, he'll be a lot more likely to make an error than if he charges and plays the ball. Taking the initiative and playing the ball will increase the odds greatly he makes the play and gets the runner out. It's the same with life. If you lie back and let life play you instead of charging forward, you're sure to experience constant mishaps and "errors." So, go make it happen; lose the weight, read more books, learn about the stock market and get out there and make it happen.

## WHAT'S YOUR VISION?

Start with your own vision. What do you want to do? What do you love to do? What are you already passionate about and how can you utilize some of your On-Time minutes daily to accomplish more in your life? When time is no longer an excuse or an obstacle, it becomes an abundant source, a powerful tool for creating more, becoming more and leading more by example. Start by waking up thirty or even just fifteen minutes earlier in the morning. Use those minutes to sit alone at the breakfast table and visualize your day.

**"Winning is a habit. Unfortunately, so is losing."** —Vince Lombardi

# 29. THE DISCIPLINE OF THE TIME

January comes from Janus, an ancient god of Roman mythology. Janus is the god of gates, doorways, beginnings and endings... and time. Most often Janus is depicted as having two faces looking in opposite directions—eastward and westward, the future and the past. Are we still living in a world of yellow yields, not seeing that January is just a word created by an ancient God of the past, controlling our minds yet still today?

Our New Year, January 1 is a time to reflect back on the year: the good, the bad, the ups, and the downs. A chance to wipe the slate clean and move in a new direction, as the clock is reset once again. This is the year I will change my ways! Unfortunately, you might have heard *the only people who like change are babies with wet diapers.*

Do we need to wait until the January 1 to put our potential to the test? I've often thought about saying, "Happy New You" or "Happy New Thoughts" on January 1 instead "Happy New Year" And why save it for January 1? Why not create new thoughts any day of the year?

*A Happy New You* happens any day of the year that you decide to change something in your life and have the discipline to stick to it!

Remember the quote, "No snowflake in the avalanche ever feels responsible." Take ownership and do your share.

If each one of us(the snowflake) in this country (the avalanche) decides to exercise for twenty minutes a day, read a book, utilize thirty minutes of their internet time for learning new skills, or just useful information that will make us smarter, faster and healthier, the country as a whole would gain and grow exponential.**It is time for the snowflakes to take accountability for their own ticket into this great game of life.**

**"It's not the work that's hard, it's the discipline."** —Anonymous

# 30. WITH GREAT POWERS COME GREAT RESPONSIBILITY

## THE HARD PART IS OVER!

- You have changed the clock by which you live your life.
- You have made the time calibration adjustments for the twenty-first century.
- You have eliminated the word "hour" from your vocabulary and are fully engaged in 1440TIME™ & The 1440 Power System®.
- You completely understand the First Wonder of the Universe, the Compound Value of Time, and you know the formula: Daily Minutes x Focused Action = Exponential Results (dm x fa = ER).
- You know it's your minutes that create your future.
- You understand the Law of Expectation, and you are expecting great things are heading your way, as that confident anticipation of the new you, has you excited about what's coming.
- You know that you can have reasons or you can have results, and you choose results.
- You know where you are on the Great Clock of Life (your GPS) and fully understand that your past does not equal your future.
- You understand that your Time Voucher is only good for 1,440 minutes today and that those minutes cannot be rolled over.

- You know that The 1440 Power System® is broken down into three zones: Sleep (you now sleep well); Livelihood (you work hard); and On-Time (the difference maker).
- You know that if you want more in your life (money, education, relationships, a healthier mind and body) it all starts in those precious On-Time minutes of your day.
- You recognize that life itself is the supreme gift (the context) and The 1440 Power System® (the content) is just the playing field. It is where you shine, prosper, and play the game to win.
- You understand that your Time Awareness System™ (TAS) has been activated and cannot be deactivated.
- You are in control of your time now—either slowing it down or speeding it up at will.

It's time… my friends. You're now ready to create the life of your dreams……

"Laissez les bons temps rouler!"

**"There is a difference between knowing the path and walking the path."**
—The Matrix, Morpheus to Neo

# APPENDIX

## Nationally, Around 76 Percent of High School Seniors Are Not Ready for College

*The New York Times stated in an article on Monday that only 23 percent of high school graduates in New York City were deemed ready to take on college or a job. In some regions in the state that number is just five percent.*

*So although NYC has a 64 percent graduation rate, more than half of those students are not* **ready for further education.**

*Nationally, around 76 percent of high school seniors are not ready for college, according to the ACT, an organization that puts out one of the most popular college entrance exams. In Utah, 74 percent are supposedly not college ready.*

**Desert News**

**Are high school seniors ready for college?**

**Published: Wednesday, Feb. 9, 2011 11:36 a.m. MST By Sara Lenz, Deseret News**

**Study says most High School seniors aren't prepared for college**

SHIAWASSEE COUNTY — A new report by the Michigan Department of Education says high school seniors in the majority of schools in Michigan—including Shiawassee County—are not prepared for college. Posted: Sunday, March 13, 2011 7:00 a.m. | *Updated: 9:59 p.m., Sat Mar 12, 2011.*

By CHRISTINA GUENTHNER, Argus-Press Staff Writer The Argus-Press |

The Truth About Senioritis *The BLOG* 01/22/2016 04:53 pm ET | Updated Jan 22, 2017

by Kate Cohen

It's the seasonal affliction that all high school seniors and parents are warned about. Many high school seniors, fresh off of winter break and finishing up the last of their college applications, begin to lag. Missing class, not doing homework, getting lower grades on assignments they would usually ace - all signs of the ever-present 'senioritis.'

Do you remember when you were a senior in high school, even if it was thirty years or more ago? For most it was a great time. You had arrived on top of the world. The freshmen, sophomores, and juniors were all envious of you. It was cool to stay up late, drive to school, or catch a ride with a friend. Classes were easy and seemed like a waste of time. It was all part of that final year Senioritis.

Think about graduating today, with high-speed Internet, Wi-Fi, Facebook, twitter, Droids, the iPhone, and the iPad. Your mind would be all over the place, just like our kids today. Now add in the media onslaught of fame, fortune, and beauty from TV and magazines. You have the perfect storm for dream land USA, a plug-and-play world of easy street America, no longer thinking of how this great country got here over the past two hundred years via blood, sweat, and tears. Parents must anticipate this problem ahead of time, get their heads out of the sand, and band together to fight this curable disease of Senioritis.

Let me introduce you to the Smart Clock, the ultimate remedy to Senioritis. The purpose is to reveal time in a way that bails out the parent.

You're not telling young adults what they can't do, but showing them how much time they really have in a day for what they can do and accomplish, all while maintaining their freedom, and use of their social electronic toys.

It is a new world and parents have to get with the program. We may not like it, but as you have already learned, the Industrial Age is over. If you don't adapt, do so at your own peril. I don't think you want your kids staying home until their thirty-five.

### "Break the habit of being you"
—Dr. Joe Dispenza D.C.

*Note: The Smart Clocks are to be used as a relative guide to lifestyle, but you must stay in the zones. You may borrow minutes from one zone to another, but the school and homework zones are constant.*

# The Smart-Clock
1440 Power System™
For seniors in High School

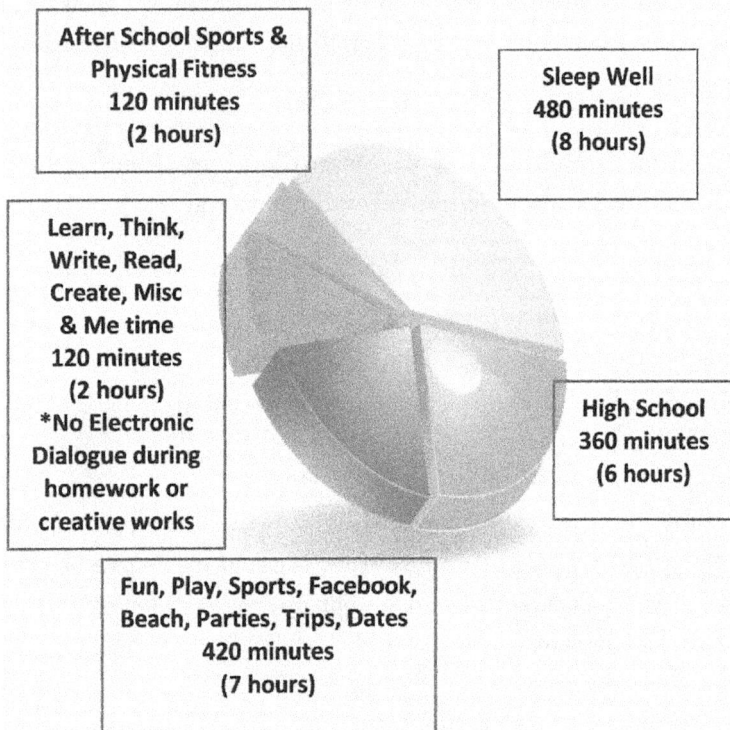

**After School Sports &
Physical Fitness
120 minutes
(2 hours)**

**Sleep Well
480 minutes
(8 hours)**

**Learn, Think,
Write, Read,
Create, Misc
& Me time
120 minutes
(2 hours)
*No Electronic
Dialogue during
homework or
creative works**

**High School
360 minutes
(6 hours)**

**Fun, Play, Sports, Facebook,
Beach, Parties, Trips, Dates
420 minutes
(7 hours)**

**"We apprehend time by making motion
-Aristotle."** —Thomas J. Watson

# The Smart-Clock
## 1440 Power System™
## College Students with No Job

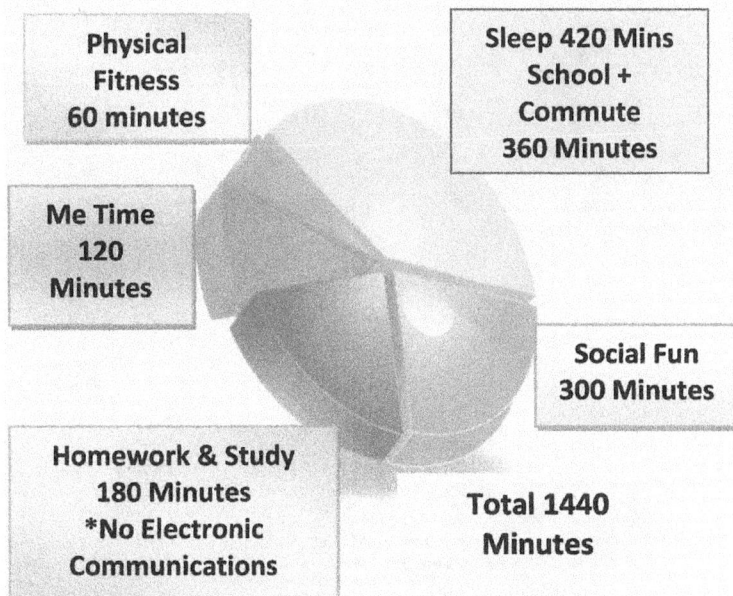

**Physical Fitness 60 minutes**

**Sleep 420 Mins School + Commute 360 Minutes**

**Me Time 120 Minutes**

**Social Fun 300 Minutes**

**Homework & Study 180 Minutes *No Electronic Communications**

**Total 1440 Minutes**

- Sleep — **7 hours**
- School four classes a day — **6 hours**
- Social and Relax Time — **5 hours**
- Home work and Study Time — **3 Hours**
- Me Time — **2 Hours**
- Fitness Time — **1 hour**

"The great dividing line between success and failure can be expressed in five words: I did not have time." —Franklin Field

## The Smart-Clock

The 1440 Power System®
College Students with a Part-Time Job (4.5 hours)

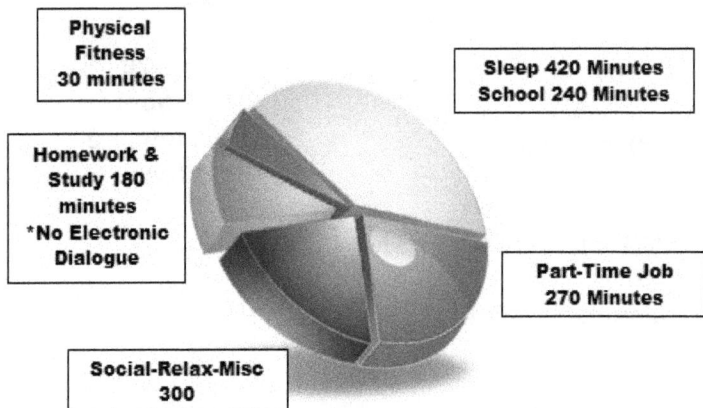

Physical
Fitness
30 minutes

Sleep 420 Minutes
School 240 Minutes

Homework &
Study 180
minutes
*No Electronic
Dialogue

Part-Time Job
270 Minutes

Social-Relax-Misc
300

| | |
|---|---|
| • Sleep | 7 hours |
| • School 3 classes + drive | 4 hours |
| • Part-time job + drive | 4.5 hours |
| • Social/Relax /Misc | 5 hours |
| • Homework & Study | 3 hours |
| • Physical Fitness | 1/2 hour |

**"It's not the work that's hard, it's the discipline."** —Anonymous

# REFERENCES FROM BOOKS, WEBSITES, ARTICLES, AND MAGAZINES

Dr. Mike Moreno The 17-Day Diet New York: Free Press, 2010
Covey, Stephen The 8th Habit: From Effectiveness to Greatness, New
York: Free Press, 2005 Mycoskie, Blake Start Something that matters
New York: Random House 2012

### Quotes used from these sites:
bobdunwoody.com, Creatingminds.org, brainyquote.com
quotegarden.com, thinkexist.com, greatquotes.com/quotes
quotationspage.com, jitteryquotes.com, gaia.com, wikinotes.com
inspirationalspark.com, world of quotes.com, wisdomquotes.com

### Websites:
Bertrand Planes Life Clocks used with permission The Life Clock
http://www.bertrandplanes.com/
Do you Know? *We are living in exponential times* vemeo.com
WikiProtest.com
NielsonWire, "*Time Spent Viewing Video on Social Networking Sites Up
98% Year-Over-Year,*"*The Nielson Company,*
*http://blog.nielsen.com/nielsenwire/online_mobile/time-spent-viewing-video-on-social-networking-sites-up-98-year-over-year-in-october/*

Average TV Viewing for 2008-09 TV Season at All-Time High
http://blog.nielsen.com/nielsenwire/media_entertainment/
average-tv-viewing-for-2008-09-tv-season-at-all-time-high/
40% of Tablet and Smartphone Owners Use Them While Watching
TV
http://blog.nielsen.com/nielsenwire/online_mobile/40-of-tablet-
and-smartphone-owners-use-them-while-watching-tv/
Nielsen reports that the time spent on social media in the US across
PCs and mobile devices increased 37 percent to 121 billion minutes
in July 2012. http://www.nielsen.com/us/en/newswire/2012/
social-media-report-2012-social-media-comes-of-age.html
*Is it live or is it Memorex?" is a trademark of Imation Corp. and its
affiliates used with permission.
http://24hourtime.blogspot.com/p/24-hour-time-system.html
A History of Timekeeping http://timekeepingsite.org/
Calendars through the Ages
http://www.webexhibits.org/calendars/week.html
September, Formerly the Seventh Month of the Roman calendar
Brian Hines Blog hinessight How to make time slow down

http://hinessight.blogs.com/hinessight/2008/01/how-to-make-
tim.html
History of the Calendar *http://www.infoplease.com/ipa/A0002061.
html*
Ancient Mythology of The Calendar http://www.squidoo.com/
ancient-myths-calendar
Wapner Scott One Nation over Weight CNBC 2011
http://www.cnbc.com/id/36073283/
http://www.nydailynews.com/entertainment/tv-movies/scott-
wapner-offers-food-thought-obesity-cnbc-nation-article-1.447908
The future of leisure time; the new value equation by Randy White, CEO

http://www.whitehutchinson.com/leisure/articles/The_future_of_leisure_time.shtml
Old Yellow Yields Sign
http://commons.wikimedia.org/wiki/File:Yellow_yield.jpg
*Calendar September, October, November, December Names of months in Latin http://wordinfo.info/unit/3197
The seven-day week comes from the seven most visible planets to man long ago—the Sun, Moon, Mercury, Venus, Mars, Saturn and Jupiter?
Wikipedia Encyclopedia
Chapter 15 Future Predictions:
http://www.futureforall.org/future-technology-predictions.html
US Department of Labor Bureau of Labor Statistics
American Time Use Survey Summery
https://www.bls.gov/tus/tables/a1_2015.pdf
http://facebookflow.com/amazing-facebook-statistics/
http://www.cnbcfix.com/review-one-nation-overweight-cnbc.html
http://www.fightchronicdisease.org/sites/fightchronicdisease.org/files/docs/CostofObesityReport-FINAL.pdf
http://healthvermont.gov/family/fit/documents/Worksite Wellness_factsheet.pdf
Factory definition: From dictionary.com
http://dictionary.reference.com/browse/factor
Are high school seniors ready for college?
Desert News
Published: Wednesday, Feb. 9, 2011 11:36 a.m. MST
By Sara Lenz, Deseret News
http://www.deseretnews.com/article/700108409/Are-high-school-seniors-ready-for-college.html
Study says most high school seniors aren't prepared for college

Posted: Sunday, March 13, 2011 7:00 a.m. | *Updated: 9:59 p.m., Sat Mar 12, 2011.* Study says most high school seniors aren't prepared for college By Christina Guenther

Argus-Press Staff Writer The Argus-Press | 9 comments

http://www.deseretnews.com/article/700108409/Are-high-school-seniors-ready-for-college.html

http://flash-clocks.com/

Provides custom and free Flash clocks for websites, blogs, iphones, ipads and more.

http://www.huffingtonpost.com/kat-cohen/truth-about-senioritis_b_9040680.html

Day 1=\$2, Day 2=\$4, Day 3=\$8, Day 4=\$16, Day 5=\$32, Day 6=\$64, Day 7=\$128, Day 8=\$256, Day 9=\$512, Day 10=\$1024 Day 11=\$2048, Day 12=\$4096, Day 13=\$8192, Day 14=\$16,384 Day 15=\$32,768, Day 16=\$65,536, Day 17=\$131,072, Day 18=\$262,144, Day 19=\$524,288, Day 20=\$100485,76

*From page 146 using a financial calculator, these are the inputs used, to get this simple time value of money answer, \$26, 304: Keystrokes: Present Value (PV) 1000, Payments (PMT) 100, Interest rate (I) 12 g i, Number of periods (N) 10 g n, Future Value (FV) answer \$26, 304.

All possible care has been taken to trace the ownership and to make full acknowledgement for its use. If any errors have occurred, they will be corrected in subsequent editions provided notification is sent to the publisher.

www.ingramcontent.com/pod-product-compliance
Lightning Source LLC
Chambersburg PA
CBHW060754050426
42449CB00008B/1400